THE ULTIMATE
DOLL BOOK

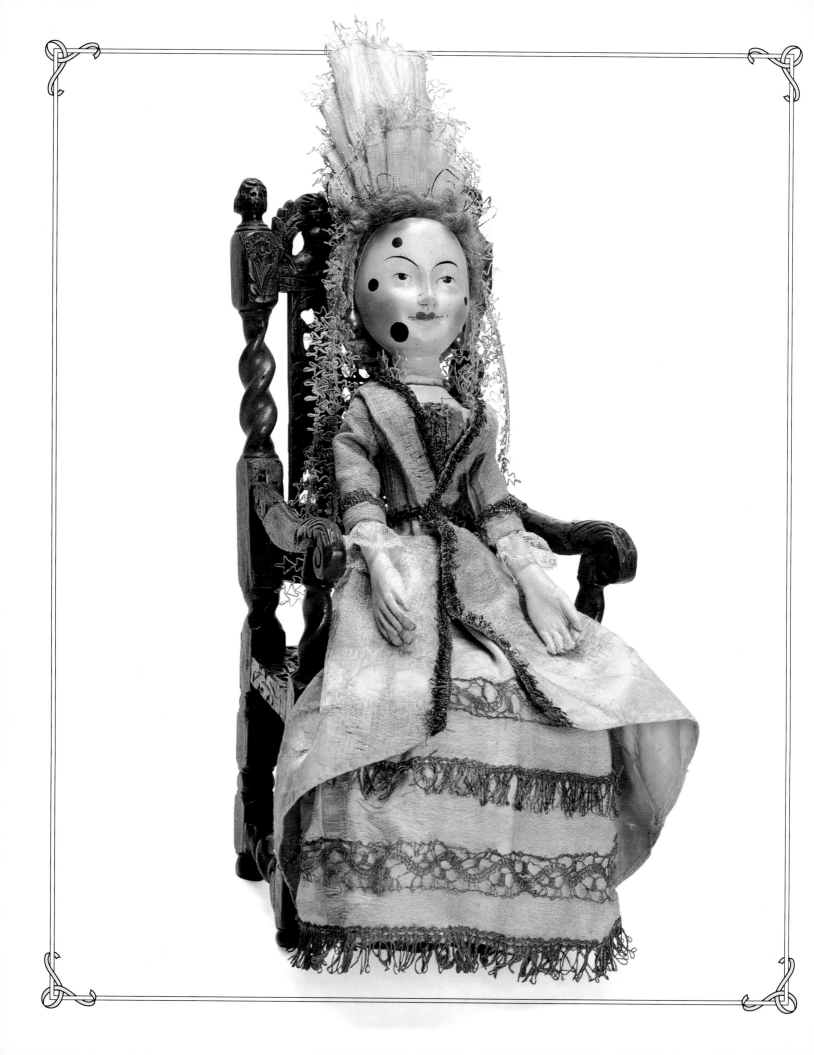

THE ULTIMATE DOLL BOOK

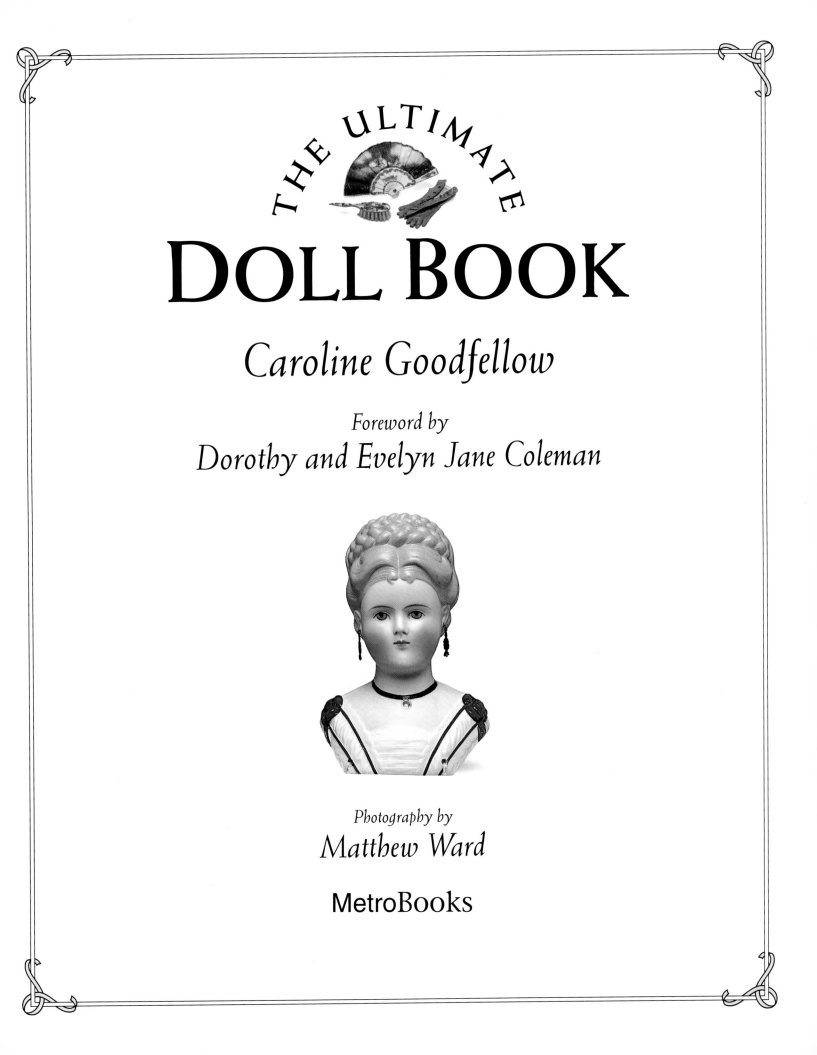

Caroline Goodfellow

Foreword by
Dorothy and Evelyn Jane Coleman

Photography by
Matthew Ward

MetroBooks

MetroBooks

This edition published by MetroBooks, an imprint of
Friedman/Fairfax Publishers, by arrangement with
Dorling Kindersley Limited, a Penguin Company

1 3 5 7 9 10 8 6 4 2
ISBN 1-58663-234-5

For bulk purchases and special sales, please contact:
Friedman/Fairfax Publishers
Attention: Sales Department
15 West 26th Street
New York, NY 10010
212/685-6610   Fax 212/685-1307

Visit our website:
www.metrobooks.com

First American Edition, 1993
Published in the United States by
Dorling Kindersley, Inc., 232 Madison Avenue
New York, New York 10016

Library of Congress Cataloging-in-Publication Data

Goodfellow, Caroline G. (Caroline Georgina)
The ultimate doll book / by Caroline Goodfellow: foreword by
Dorothy and Evelyn Jane Coleman -- 1st American ed.

p. cm.
Includes index.
ISBN 1-58663-234-5
1. Dolls--History. I. Title.

NK4894.A2G66 1993

688.7'221'09--dc20   92-30516
                                                      CIP

Computer page makeup by
Cooling Brown Partnership, Great Britain
Text film output by The Right Type, Great Britain
Reproduced by Colourscan, Singapore
Printed and bound in Slovakia by TBB

Descriptions of the dolls on these pages can be
found in the appropriate sections of the book.
On page 1: *"Solid Comfort" (see p.88)*. On page 2:
"Old Pretender" (see p.13). On page 3: *Patterned
Shoulder Head (see p.49)*. On page 4: *"Harry the
Hawk" (see p.103)*. On page 5 top: *Mandarin with
Long Fingers (see p.135)*.

Contents

PORCELAIN PARADE (BELOW) This selection of nine bisque and untinted bisque dolls illustrates the fine craftsmanship of French and German doll-makers in the late 19th and early 20th centuries.

Foreword

Dorothy and Evelyn Jane Coleman

GLAZED CHINA DOLL
(BELOW) *This fine example from the Coleman Collection was made in Germany between 1865 and 1870, and has the typically classical look that was so fashionable at that time. The shoulder plate has a molded, decorated design. The body is of stuffed cloth, with kid lower arms. Ht: 20in (50cm)*

EVEN IN THE DAYS of the early Greeks, dolls were part of domestic life, and since then they have played a significant role in almost every civilization. Today, collecting dolls is a prominent, popular pursuit worldwide: everywhere, dolls are objects of great interest and desirability.

〜 It has been our good fortune to visit numerous museums and private collections of dolls throughout the world. What a thrill it is to see the early native dolls in Alaska, the many dolls of the Americas, the Australian dolls, and of course, the dolls in Europe. Recently, we revisited Thuringia, in Germany, where the majority of the dolls in our collection were originally produced. Sadly, its once-prosperous doll-making industry has almost ceased to exist, but the antique dolls themselves live on in public displays and individual collections.

Looking at Dolls

In 1992, during our second visit to Australia, we gave many talks on dolls, including a program of lectures at the Powerhouse Museum in Sydney. Some of the people attending had traveled long distances just to be there. While we were at the museum, the curator showed some of the dolls that had been brought to Australia in the distant past. Most had never before been seen by the public, and not even by doll collectors in Australia. We were not certain which gave them the greater pleasure: was it the very special privilege of seeing these dolls that had come to Australia long ago, or the rare opportunity of viewing our color slides of different and exciting dolls from around the world?
〜 Fortunately, one does not always have to travel a great distance in order to see pictures of beautiful dolls. Readers of *The Ultimate Doll Book* can look at, study, and enjoy some of the dolls that belong to

"LADY BETTY MODISH"
(ABOVE) *This elegant, c.1902 Kestner bisque-headed doll (see pages 74–75) is one of the major exhibits at the Wenham Museum. Ht: 17½in (45cm)*

major private collections such as Faith Eaton's, in England, and our own, in the United States: both of these have been decades in the making. *The Ultimate Doll Book* also provides wonderful photographs of dolls from London's Bethnal Green Museum of Childhood (a branch of the Victoria & Albert Museum) and in the United States, the Wenham Historical Association and Museum, in Massachusetts. These two museums have outstanding collections of dolls; some of the dolls date back many years, or even centuries.

The World of the Collector

Once you buy a doll, hopefully you will live with it for many years; as you learn more about it, your doll may become an even greater treasure. Seek dolls in as original condition as possible, not ones that have been repaired or altered. Be sure the clothes are of about the same period as the doll, too. Examine and familiarize yourself with the marks and every detail of their heads, bodies, and clothes, especially the shoes. This can tell you a considerable amount about your dolls, such as who made them and where – and perhaps, when – they were made.

Frauds and Fakes

Dolls are often put together at various stages of their lives. For example, the head could be purchased and the rest of the doll made at home; parts may have been replaced at a doll hospital; or dealers today can put parts of different ages together to create a doll. If a doll that appeals to you has been altered and wears recently made clothes, wait until you can find a similar doll, but in its original condition, including the wig and the costume.

Future Preservation

Millions and millions of dolls with bisque heads were made in the nineteenth and early twentieth centuries, yet only a few have survived intact. Their modern, porcelain relatives – now often produced as collectors' dolls rather than toys – do not have to suffer the same harsh treatment. They are handled with care, so that they will be available for years to come. Now, many of the dolls of old are being given similar consideration. At least a few surviving old dolls, as well as some newer ones, can be enjoyed in *The Ultimate Doll Book*, and thus provide pleasure for this and future generations.

WAX-OVER-COMPOSITION (ABOVE) *Made in the mid-19th century in England or Germany, this doll from the Faith Eaton Collection has a wax-over-papier-mâché shoulder head, cloth body and upper arms and legs, and kid lower arms. Ht: 31in (80cm)*

WATERCOLOR MINIATURE (ABOVE) *One of a group of miniatures, "The Four Whitmore Children," by 18th-century artist Paul-Peter Lens shows a girl holding a contemporary doll.*

PIEROTTI DOLL (BELOW) *Made by Pierotti in England in the early 20th century, this lady is exhibited at the Bethnal Green Museum of Childhood. It has a poured wax shoulder head and lower arms and legs. The skill of the maker is evident in the fine modeling and graceful pose of the doll's hands. Ht: 16in (41cm)*

Introducing Dolls

ASK TEN DIFFERENT PEOPLE "What is a doll?" and you will probably get as many different answers, each one qualified by the period, culture, and society that have formed and shaped that person's singular perception of the world. Yet, crossing all barriers of individual perspective and time, race, and class, we discover the generally accepted idea of what a doll is: an inanimate object that represents a human being in miniature.

In *The Ultimate Doll Book*, we have chosen to focus on dolls intended for use as playthings. Of course, there are many other types of dolls: dolls' house dolls and paper dolls, marionettes and puppets, to name just a few. All these are quite separate subjects in their own right. Vying for attention with the play dolls featured in this book, they would not have received the closely detailed pictorial and textual commentary they deserve.

Although all the dolls illustrated and described in these pages were made within the past 300 years, our knowledge of ancient civilizations leads us directly to the assumption that dolls did not suddenly appear in the seventeenth century but had evolved to that point over thousands of years. A swift trip through *The Ultimate Doll Book* reveals a continuing ebb and flow to this process of gradual evolution, as new materials and innovative manufacturing techniques have changed the course of doll-making history.

GIRL WITH A DOLL (ABOVE) *This oil-on-canvas painting, entitled "Portrait of Lilly, Daughter of J. Noble, Esq.," is the work of English artist Sir John Everett Millais, who lived between 1826 and 1896. The figure held by the child shows an example of the gorgeously dressed lady dolls that were made in France in the later years of this period.*

C. 1915 CHARCOAL SELLER (BELOW) *Created in the United States by one of the Vargus family of New Orleans, this wax doll represents a "Cry" of the city. Cries, which portray familiar trades and occupations, usually take the form of pictures rather than three-dimensional objects. Ht: 7in (18cm)*

Dolls as Playthings

The use to which dolls have been put over the years has varied enormously, from religious offerings at one end of the spectrum to playthings at the other. But the majority of the dolls produced between 1680 and the 1990s – the time period covered by our book – were almost certainly intended to be used as children's playthings. Many were designed for a particular age group: in the eighteenth century, simple rag dolls, stitched and stuffed by mothers using any readily available household materials, were generally made as comfort toys for young babies and children under five.

In England, older middle-class children had "Sunday only" dolls, which were taken out to be played with under strict adult supervision for an hour or two in the afternoon. The elegantly attired, bisque-headed fashion dolls and those with elaborately molded hairstyles, made in France and Germany in the latter half of the nineteenth century, fall into this category.

∽ Since the 1930s, more and more dolls have been mass-produced, particularly in the United States. Faced with rising costs and the whims of a must-have buying public, manufacturers target niche markets as a matter of survival, ensuring a good return on their capital outlay and investment.

Chronology and Order

The ten sections of *The Ultimate Doll Book* are arranged so that the materials from which dolls have been made are described as they were first used for this purpose, in a loosely knit chronology. History is not so neatly ordered, however, that one section begins where the previous section came to an end: doll-makers did not stop using one material simply because another became available.

∽ Some materials, such as wood, have stepped backward in their "evolution." Others, for example bisque, have been superseded by newer ones. Even within the bounds of this scenario, a material can be rediscovered, perhaps in a novel form. Individual doll-makers are now using a ceramic-like art clay called Sculpey, formulated in the United States, to create doll heads with the look of fine bisque porcelain.

∽ Manufacturing innovations have played their part in the story as well. Realistically modeled plastic dolls would scarcely be possible without the techniques of injection molding that were developed in the 1940s. For some, such technology allows realism to be carried to unpalatable extremes: Villy Nielsen's Judith "Mother and Baby" – a doll with a spring-loaded abdominal cavity that "gives birth" to a tiny baby – and Effe's male-sexed *Bimbovero* are not to everyone's taste.

The Language of Dolls

Remember, as you read *The Ultimate Doll Book*, that unfamiliar words, or familiar words used in unfamiliar ways, are just a means of identifying the different types of dolls. Transported into nineteenth-century France, "doll" becomes *bébé* (baby) for dolls representing young children as well as babies, and *poupée* (doll) for older child and adult dolls – confusing stuff for newcomers who might assume that a French *bébé Jumeau* is a Jumeau baby doll. But learning the special language of dolls is all part of the fun of discovering this fascinating subject.

GIRL SCOUT OF AMERICA
(*ABOVE*) *This 1950s' Vogue Dolls, Inc. Ginny is typical of the hard plastic dolls made after World War II. Ht: 7in (18cm)* Vogue Dolls® is a registered trademark of Dakin, Inc. All Vogue Dolls designs © 1993 Dakin, Inc., Woodland Hills, California, USA, reproduced here courtesy of Dakin.

RUSSIAN NESTING DOLL, YELTSIN (*BELOW*) *The correct term for these brightly painted wooden dolls is* matryoshka. *The dolls fit inside one another and are usually made in series of between six and ten figures. Ht: 4¼in (11cm)*

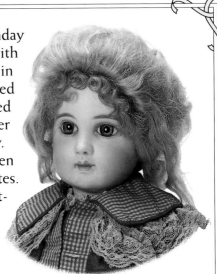

BÉBÉ JUMEAU (*ABOVE*)
Large, bulbous eyes are a feature of early Jumeau dolls. This one is described in extensive detail on page 58. Doll ht: 22in (55cm)

1980S GERMAN DOLL
(*BELOW*) *The original wrist tag bears the legend "Stupsi, your lovable cuddly companion." A bendable soft vinyl doll, Stupsi has a soft and cozy covering of stockinette. Ht: 17in (43cm)*

Wooden Dolls

Inexpensive and readily available, wood has always been used for making dolls. Wooden dolls with any accurately documented history date from c. 1680, although they were, of course, made before this time. A few figures have been found in ancient burial sites, yet genuine examples of very early dolls have all but disappeared – destroyed, perhaps as idolatrous images during times of religious conflict, or simply deemed not worth keeping.

RECORDS DOCUMENTING DOLL-MAKING activities show that of the dolls surviving from the 1600s and 1700s, the majority – or even all – are English. Most are made of pine, a wood that was in plentiful supply, easy to carve or turn on a lathe, but also able to withstand rough treatment. As with other types of doll, a great number of wooden dolls were made by parents for their children, but the most

LADY AND LORD CLAPHAM (*LEFT and RIGHT*) *These two carved wooden dolls wear "Fashionable Undress" – costumes so typical of the late 17th-century English upper class that they date the pair c. 1690. The similarity between the dolls suggests that they are probably the work of a single maker. Both are fully painted over a gesso base and have painted eyes and facial features. Ht: 19in (48cm)*

accomplished examples are almost certainly the work of professional carvers, making dolls for sale.

In Europe, the toy-making industry (which also produced dolls) evolved over more than two hundred years. By the 1600s, it was established as an organized craft guild alongside other guilds that embraced similarly traditional skills. This indicates that doll-making existed in Europe long before the end of the eighteenth century, when dolls attributed to European makers came onto the market. In the Grödener Tal region of Austria (now a part of Italy) and in Oberammergau, Berchtesgaden, and Sonneberg, three small German towns, rich forests of pine provided abundant raw materials for making dolls. The town of Erzgebirge, near Dresden, was another energetic wooden toy-making center.

Early Dolls

The early wooden dolls – those made between 1680 and 1720 – are considered to be carefully crafted. Each has the head and torso carved as one, and shows a distinctly individual facial expression, with painted or inset glass eyes, and noses, mouths, and ears which are well defined. Their limbs are attached by various pinning and jointing methods, according to the material. The upper arms are most usually made of bound

PEG WOODENS POSTCARD
(*RIGHT*) *During the 1890s, Bertha Upton wrote a series of children's books, illustrated by her daughter, Florence. The series inspired a line of merchandise, including card games and postcards. The adventures of two peg wooden dolls (and their friend, Golliwogg) were some of their most popular stories.*

GRÖDENER TAL SHOULDER HEADS
(*ABOVE and RIGHT*) *Sometimes known as Wooden Bettys, and now rather rare, heads such as these inexpensive 1930s designs were mass-produced from 1880 to 1940, mainly for export. They are crudely carved and painted, and are usually attached to coarse cloth bodies. Ht: 4in (10cm)*

linen, while the lower parts are made of carved wood. Fingers and thumbs are separate and many examples display fingernail detail. Wood was usually used for the upper and lower legs. The feet tend to be skillfully made, with well-carved toes and toenails. The whole body was covered with a base layer of gesso first, then delicately painted, and finally varnished. The finished dolls were dressed in stylish costumes of the period.

A Retrograde Development

After 1720, wooden dolls deteriorated rather than improving in quality. A more stylized, less individual appearance is conveyed in the dolls' flattened faces and facial features. The painstaking carving of the earlier doll bodies gave way to a roughly fashioned torso and limbs, although the narrow-waisted, broad-hipped shape was retained. As before, the wooden limbs and knee joints were attached to the torso with pegged tongue and groove joints. When all-wooden arms had replaced the earlier linen-and-wooden type, tongue and groove joints were also applied to the shoulders and elbows. Despite the relatively unrefined workmanship, the joints themselves are surprisingly efficient, allowing easy mobility for the arms and legs. Ball joints were used for some 1800s dolls, giving them the look of an artist's mannequin or lay figure, and providing their limbs with even greater freedom of movement than the tongue and groove joints.

Finishing techniques were also less sophisticated than those of earlier dolls. The gesso base layer was still used, but paint was applied only to the face and upper torso – areas that were meant to resemble naked "flesh" – while the rest of the body was left white. Toward the end of the 1700s, even the gesso layer was abandoned, and doll bodies were unpainted, showing the bare wood.

The overall decline in the quality of wooden dolls continued into the nineteenth and twentieth centuries. They were generally considered throwaway items, and their appearance only helped to support this view. However, once again, some of the dolls did exhibit the individual personality of the 1680s dolls, as we can observe in the work of such fine craftsmen as the innovative American dollmakers Joel Ellis (see page 14) and Albert Schoenhut (see page 15).

LUCKY MASCOT (*LEFT*) *Small wooden dolls were once peddled at the Derby – a classic fixture of the English racing season – and worn in the hatband for good luck. Sir John Everett Millais's pen and ink drawing of 1853 pokes fun at a couple's despair after losing a bet.*

Early Dolls

· 1680s to 1820s ·

MOST EARLY WOODEN DOLLS were made in England, probably in and around London, by a number of different makers. Fewer than 30 seventeenth-century English wooden dolls have survived. Female dolls far outnumber males, which have the same shape, but are dressed in masculine attire. The formal appearance and fashionable clothing of both types suggests that they were made for adults, rather than as children's playthings.

Dolls of this period are often called "Queen Anne" dolls – a misnomer, because most were made either before 1702 or after 1714, the years of her reign. Dating these rare, virtually priceless dolls is difficult. The clothes, usually sewn to the body, do not allow examination of the naked figure, which would reveal clues to the doll's age.

Curly human hair wig, nailed to head

Lathe-turned head and torso are painted in flesh tones over a gesso base

Separate, carved fingers are often broken off or damaged

Legs and lower torso are painted white over a gesso base

Linen upper arms

Wooden lower arms

Wooden peg

Tongue-and-groove joints, with wooden pegs, at knees and hips

Roughly shaped feet have no toes

HT: 16in (41cm)

Head and torso made from one block of wood, turned on a lathe and carved

Dark brown glass eyes, embedded in slots cut in the face

Torso has a rounded chest, narrow waist, flat back, and broad, squarish hips

Sleeves conceal linen upper arms, stitched to torso through holes drilled in shoulders

Silk damask winter dress with lace trim

Carved, separate flat fingers and thumbs on wooden lower arms

Dress conceals linen, wool-embroidered petticoat and linen undergarments

Lower arms are covered with kid gloves

AUGUSTA MARIANNA (ABOVE) This c.1780 lady is typical of dolls made after 1760. It lacks the finely modeled features of earlier dolls, an example of which can be seen on the right. Ht: 19in (48cm)
1745 DOLL (RIGHT) The well-defined nose, mouth, lozenge-shaped eyes, and brows and lashes (indicated with dots of paint) give this figure a definite personality.

Bulbous glass eyes, slotted into face

Well-defined nose, ears, and mouth

Head and narrow-waisted torso carved from one piece of wood

Shaped and painted breasts

Finely carved hands show rounded fingers with fingernails

Original linen upper arms have been rebound and nailed to the shoulders

Hips are carved on each side to house tongues from leg joints

Wide-hipped lower torso, shaped at back to suggest buttocks

Carved, but not separate, toes

Lower legs have fine calves and ankles

EUROPEAN RIVAL, C.1820
(RIGHT) From the end of the 18th century, cheaper German dolls competed with the expensive English models. They were painted directly onto the wood, on areas that would show: the costly gesso base layer was entirely omitted. Ht: 8½in (22cm)

Painted hair, eyes, and mouth

Wedge, inserted into face, forms nose

Limbs are attached to torso with wooden pegs

UNCLOTHED MODEL (ABOVE) This doll, made between 1700 and 1720, is remarkable in its relatively close resemblance to the human form. Its unclothed state provides a rare opportunity to study the maker's craftsmanship. Ht: 19in (48cm)

1680s carved walnut and cane chair, styled after full-sized chairs in Holyroodhouse

Head and body, carved from separate pieces of wood, are gessoed and painted

Painted eyes, a feature of many early dolls

Black beauty patches were the height of fashion

"FASHIONABLE UNDRESS FOR SPRING 1755" (RIGHT) In the mid-1700s, a young English girl, Laetitia Clark Powell, created doll costumes based on dresses she had once worn herself. This costume, made when she was 13, is worn by a typical, stylized wooden doll. Ht: 11in (28cm)

Human hair wig

Brown glass eyes

Painted facial features

Cloth covers wooden lower arms, to look like gloves

Kid-covered hands appear large, but are in proportion to head

Informal "at-home" costume made of silk brocade

"OLD PRETENDER" (ABOVE) The attire, face patches, and known history of this doll suggest it was made c.1680. It is said that it belonged to the court of King James II at Holyroodhouse in Edinburgh, Scotland. Ht: 21in (53cm)

Dolls from the New World

· 1850s to 1930s ·

IN THE UNITED STATES, New England was the creative center for toy- and doll-making in the mid-nineteenth century. Many American makers were by this time already established producers of wooden toys, but their doll designs, though innovative, were often unsuccessful: the buying public, composed largely of recently settled Europeans, found dolls of the familiar European style and type more to its taste (see pages 18–19). Some early American dolls were the work of individuals, made in their spare time; other makers progressed to form companies that manufactured dolls on a grander scale. By the twentieth century, makers were often immigrants who had worked with toys or dolls in their native land, and the making of dolls had spread beyond New England to many other parts of the country.

Hair is usually brownish black; blond hair is rare

Molded facial features are hand-painted

Dowel rod attaches rigid head to body

Head and neck are painted to resemble skin

Mortise and tenon joints at shoulders give full articulation

Upper torso is painted yellow

Mortise and tenon joints at elbows

Stiffened cotton apron, with printed "embroidery" in a traditional design

Hands and wrists are made of cast lead, painted cream

Mortise and tenon joints at hips

A metal pin secures each mortise and tenon joint

Flesh-toned paint on lower legs

Cast lead feet and ankles, painted to resemble boots

Hand-painted drawstring purse, tied to wrist

Bloomers trimmed with intricate cotton tatting

HT: 15in (38cm)

JOEL ELLIS, 1873 PATENTED DOLL *The Co-operative Manufacturing Co. produced these dolls for the Vermont Novelty Works, founded in 1858 by Joel Ellis, Rodney Britton, and Ellis Eaton in Springfield, Massachusetts. Ellis's doll has a rock maple head, steamed and shaped in a hydraulic press, and lead hands and feet.*

KENTUCKY MOUNTAIN PAIR
(RIGHT) Dating from the 1930s, this pair is thought to be the work of one person making dolls as a hobby, rather than a company. The male figure is distinguished from the female essentially by its clothes, and in small details such as the hair and body padding. Ht: 10in (25cm)

Brown, poor-quality mohair wig, stuck to head

Solid wood head, with crudely carved facial features

Cheeks and chin are stained with pink ink or water-based paint

Cloth-over-wood padded upper torso

Wooden lower and upper arms

Eyes, lashes, and brows are defined with pencil

Female figure has no padding

Both dolls have a handwritten ink mark on the upper back that reads "Hall," probably the name of the maker.

HALL

SCHOENHUT ALL-WOOD PERFECTION ART DOLL
(BELOW) Albert Schoenhut, a German immigrant, started trading in Philadelphia, Pennsylvania, in 1872. In 1911, his company was awarded a patent for an all-wood doll with metal spring joints. The unique flexible jointing system allows much movement, but is rigid enough for the doll to be posed without falling over. Ht: 16in (40cm)

Hair is molded with the head and painted yellowish blond

Head turns a full 360°

Suit conceals stuffed cloth upper legs and lower torso

Wooden lower legs, with blue ink- or paint-stained feet

Solid wood head

Mortise and tenon joints, with wooden pegs, at shoulders and hips

Rock maple body, unpainted on parts likely to be clothed

Dress conceals feet, which are almost identical to the man's

Joints at elbows, neck, shoulders, wrists, hips, knees, and ankles

Ball and socket joints at knees and elbows

The mark is pressed into the upper back of the doll. This model was made until 1939.

JOINTED DOLL COMPANY
(LEFT) This doll has ball and socket joints patented by George W. Sanders, and a composition-over-wood head, patented by Charles C. Johnson. It was produced and distributed by the Jointed Doll Co., Springfield, Vermont, c.1880. Ht: 12in (30cm)

Cast lead feet, painted blue to represent boots

Oblique hole allows doll to hold foot in tiptoe position

Straight hole allows doll to hold the foot resting flat

15

Poupards and Simple Dolls

· 1800s to the present day ·

NOT ALL OF THE EARLIEST DOLLS were as sophisticated as the elegant individuals shown on pages 12 and 13. Stump dolls (simple, one-piece figures, carved from a block of wood) were produced during the same period in England and Germany. The majority were quite roughly made, although some had intricate painted decoration that showed the type of clothing worn by fashionable ladies. Poupards succeeded stump dolls and came mainly from the Erzgebirge region of Germany. These legless (arms were an occasional feature) figures were crudely carved or turned on a lathe, then painted in bright colors. Poupards usually represent babies in swaddling clothes, or men and women. Twentieth-century versions sometimes have the added refinement of jointed heads and arms or sound mechanisms. Other types of simple dolls are those made from wooden spoons or old-fashioned straight clothespins, materials that remain firm favorites with makers even today.

Carved grooves give texture to painted hair

Nose is a triangular wedge of wood, inserted into a slit in the face

Crudely painted mouth

Painted wavy line around neck, suggesting lace trim on the swaddling

Painted hair continues around back of doll's head

Doll's name and origin, handwritten in pencil in German script, "Thÿmiane/die Düftende/geboren zu/Sterzing/20. Juli 1926" (Thÿmiane/the Aromatic One/born in/Sterzing/20 July 1926)

Doll is roughly carved from one piece of wood, with smoother finish on head and torso

Painted floral decoration is applied over the body base color

Flat back has been left unpainted

Lower part of inscription is illegible

THE "AROMATIC ONE" Thÿmiane die Düftende is the female half of a pair of large poupards. According to the pencil inscriptions on their backs, the doll and its male companion, the "Awkward One" – Schnattissimo der Rüpel – were "born" in the German village of Sterzing on July 20th, 1926. Both figures are painted, on the front only, to represent young babies swaddled, or wrapped, in cloth strips, in the traditional fashion.

Front of figure is painted with flesh tones, now faded to cream

HT: 11in (28cm)

Face and upper torso are painted in flesh tones

Unjointed wooden arms, pegged to torso at shoulders

Painted lower arms are unvarnished

Legs end in roughly shaped painted shoes

Sides of bobbed hair are shaped as part of the head and defined with paint

The mark is screen-printed on the back of the head, over the painted hair.

CLOTHESPIN DOLL (RIGHT)
Straight, old-fashioned clothespins were often transformed by mothers into improvised playthings. The raffia hair of this c.1955 doll is ingeniously bound to fall on either side of its neck, so that the plaits form the doll's arms. Ht: 4½in (11.5cm)

Mouth and eyes are drawn with ballpoint pen

Metal rivets join limbs to torso

Clothes are made from rag-bag scraps of cotton material

Wood has been neither painted nor varnished

1920s PEG WOODEN (ABOVE)
Large numbers of cheap dolls were produced in Grödener Tal throughout the 1800s. The 20th-century version shown here differs from them only in its "flapper" costume. Ht: 6in (15cm)

WOMAN WITH HAT (BELOW)
Poupards with arms usually represent adults. This German doll was made between 1900 and 1930, but is based on an old design. Ht: 6in (15cm)

Legs and arms have limited sideways and up-and-down movement

HAPPY DAYS GIRL (LEFT)
This 1930s English doll is made from flat pieces of wood, painted and varnished to show facial features, hair, and feet. The simple fixings at the shoulders and hips hold the arms and legs in place, and provide an effective, if basic, jointing system. Ht: 8in (20cm)

Penciled eyes, nostrils, and mouth

Carved nose

1920s FLAPPER (BELOW) This wooden spoon shows how household equipment can be transformed with a little imagination. Painted in black on white, with touches of red and gold, it is a stylish impression of a flapper. Ht: 12in (30cm)

Slots in body sides allow arms to be raised and lowered

Arms, carved as wide sleeves, are of a piece with the body

Lathe-turned doll, made in 1983

Original poupard design, reinterpreted by a modern maker

1991 POUPARD (ABOVE) This fine piece of wood-turning is the work of doll artist Elizabeth Pongratz. Ht: 5½in (14cm)

BAVARIAN BABY (LEFT) A small doll has been decorated with oil-based paints. Ht: 3½in (9cm)

Dress, made of black nylon upholstery fringe, "dances" when spoon handle is twirled

Convex sides of spoons form feet

TOMMY SPOONER (ABOVE) This character, made in the United States c.1896, is constructed from five wooden spoons attached to a carved, hollowed-out body. The legend on its back — "Pack carefully, do not handle" — may have been added at a later date. Ht: 12in (30cm)

Peg Woodens

· 1790s to the present day ·

JOINTED WOODEN DOLLS made after 1790 are usually called Dutch dolls or peg woodens. The first term may be a corruption of *deutsch*, meaning German – indicating their country of origin – or a reference to the Dutch ports through which they were exported from Germany to England. The second term refers to the use of pegs in the jointing and the fact that the dolls resemble straight, old-fashioned clothespins. Regardless of terminology, these dolls are united in being relatively simple turned and carved figures, which were usually painted only on the parts that were unclothed. ⁓ Although World War II created a hiatus in the large-scale production of peg woodens, a recent awakening of interest in the old techniques, together with improved machinery and paints, has given these inexpensive dolls a new lease on life today.

The printed label, sewn into the dress, indicates that this doll was made in 1963 as a favor to mark the annual Convention of the United Federation of Doll Clubs, held in the United States.

Head and torso are carved as one unit

High carved comb on top of head

Head and chest area are finished with flesh-toned paint

Painted hair and facial features

Joints are neater than those on similar 19th-century dolls

Simply carved hands have thumbs but no fingers

Torso is shaped into broad, flat hips and a narrow waist

Straight, unshaped thighs

Doll wears a dress in the style of a young lady of the late 19th century

Lower legs have rounded calves and trim ankles

Mortise and tenon joints attach limbs to torso and give movement to lower legs and arms

Dainty black slippers are painted onto the feet

Lower legs are painted to show white stockings

TUCKCOMB DOLL, "ANGELITA" *Hand-crafted in the United States by S. Smith, this fully jointed peg wooden is a modern version of an 1850s German doll. The high comb, often painted yellow, was a fashionable hair ornament of that period. It is carved as one with the head, and is a special feature of early 19th-century wooden dolls.*

HT: 6½in (16.5cm)

Ht: 17in (43cm)

Largest doll has ball joints at shoulders and hips

PEG WOODEN PARADE (LEFT)
This set was produced in the Grödener Tal region of Austria between 1925 and 1940. The largest figure has a relatively sophisticated jointing system, and even the tiniest of the nine has peg joints at the shoulders and hips.

PONYTAIL PEG DOLL (RIGHT)
The decorative tuckcomb, a feature of early 19th-century, Grödener Tal-made peg woodens, has been reinterpreted in this c. 1960 version and updated as a carved ponytail. It was made by English collector Faith Eaton. Ht: 5in (13cm)

Facial features and hair are painted over base of flesh-colored oils

Ht: 12in (30cm)

All dolls have painted black hair, blue eyes, and red mouths

Ht: 10in (25cm)

Clothing conceals torso, carved from same piece of wood as the head

Noses of three largest dolls made of wooden wedge, slotted into the face

Ht: 6¾in (17cm)

Mortise and tenon joints at hips, shoulders, elbows, and knees

Noses of middle-sized dolls are painted; smaller dolls have no nose

Ht: 4¼in (11cm)

Ht: 3¼in (8cm)

Ht: 1¾in (4.5cm)

Ht: 1in (2.5cm)

Ht: ⅝in (1.5cm)

Lower legs are sticklike, but still have painted shoe detail

Feet are always painted to represent shoes

DOLL MOUNTED AS AN ORNAMENTAL PIN (ABOVE) *This early 1960s miniature peg wooden was made by S. Smith in the United States. It has a carved comb on top of the head and a safety pin on the back of the frame. Ht: 1in (2.5cm)*

1820s PEG WOODEN (BELOW)
Peasants in the Grödener Tal carved dolls like this one during the harsh winter months, when they could not work in the forests. Though made in quantity, each doll has its own special features. Ht: 3½in (9cm)

Fully jointed doll is encased in glass-fronted wooden frame

Original coarse cotton dress, shawl, and apron

DOLL DRESSED AS A NUN
(RIGHT) *Many of these cheap dolls were clothed to represent figures from everyday life. In 1920s rural Austria, nuns were very much part of the Catholic communities. Ht: 6in (15cm)*

Rounded head, with an elongated neck

Flat arms have simple peg joints at the elbows

Hand-painted facial features

Woolen wimple and habit

Glass rosary beads, with a metal crucifix

Composition Dolls

The collective term "composition" is used to describe a variety of pulped wood- or paper-based mixtures from which doll heads and bodies are made. Originally introduced as a less expensive alternative to wood, composition also had the advantage of being a more malleable material. Toward the end of the eighteenth century, exciting experiments took place in the development of papier-mâché – the doll industry's most favored type of composition.

FROM THE START, manufacturers found that the papier-mâché mixture could be pressed into molds for shaping. The revolutionary idea – which sprang to life in the 1800s, and had far-reaching effects for doll-making – was to mold the mixture *under pressure*. Treated in this way, papier-mâché was found to be a strong, durable material that lent itself easily to mass production by machine. This versatility could now be exploited to fashion a wide range of products other than doll parts, including ornaments, boxes, and furniture. After molding, a glutinous wash called size was applied to the objects. This eliminated the need for the expensive gesso layer that was used with wood (see page 11) and prepared an even ground for paint.

Manufacturers took great pride in developing their own specially formulated papier-mâché mixtures and kept the recipes a closely guarded secret. A variety of bizarre ingredients might be added to the basic pulp – rags, bread, crushed eggshells, or ground-up animal bones or bone ash, for example – that increased the strength of the molded material while reducing its raw cost. As most recipes were not recorded or patented, the precise formula of the composition mixture used for a particular doll is invariably unknown and can only be determined by expensive chemical analysis.

Getting the Formula Right

Other types of composition, still based on wood or paper, were developed from the mid-nineteenth century. The increased use of additives such as glue, flour, boiled sawdust, plaster, and anything else that was affordable and available, did not always produce a result that was as indestructible as the manufacturers claimed. Composition containing edible ingredients attracted rodents and insects; other mixtures were affected by temperature and humidity, and would swell or shrink according to changes in the weather.

∽ Papier-mâché was the unrivaled success of all the experimentation, and became the most widely used type of composition for doll heads and, somewhat later, bodies. Its first practical application was in the making of shoulder heads; papier-mâché socket heads followed later, introduced in the third quarter of the nineteenth century. But papier-mâché composition really came into its own with the development of

COTTAGE INDUSTRY *(LEFT)*
The processes required to finish machine-made composition heads and limbs were usually carried out as piecework by families in their own homes. In this engraving, the man is painting the heads, while the woman is dressing the completed doll.

1850S GIRL (RIGHT) *Most wax-over-composition dolls were made in Germany. This doll has a wax-over-papier-mâché shoulder head and lower limbs, with a stuffed cloth torso and upper limbs. With its auburn mohair wig, sleeping glass eyes, and period costume, this doll is a fine example of its type. Ht: 12in (30cm)*

the original color tones changes, and the surface is left exposed and vulnerable to damage.

From the turn of the twentieth century onward, the material that had started out as a cheap substitute for wood and then bisque increased in popularity with manufacturers in both France and Germany. And in the United States – a country that had no tradition of making bisque dolls – composition was used for almost all dolls until it was superseded by modern plastics, such as polyethylene and vinyl, in the 1940s.

Wax-over-composition

The process of coating composition heads with a layer of wax to enhance the appearance of the doll heads evolved almost as soon as manufacturers realized the potential of machine-molding papier-mâché mixtures. This technique was used with other types of composition, along with other materials, but was found to be most successful when applied to papier-mâché composition. Unfortunately, one principal disadvantage of wax-over-composition was soon revealed: an unsightly deterioration in the smooth surface of the wax. Caused by the different rates at which the two layers of composition and wax expanded and contracted, this produced faults ranging from fine-line crazing to wide cracks. Manufacturers were never able to solve this problem. As a result, the production of wax-over-composition doll parts came to an end during the first decade of the twentieth century.

doll bodies, in particular those with jointed limbs. Its strength, durability, and lightness, as well as suitability for molding, enabled manufacturers to make a range of different body types. Thin wooden slats provided additional strength for the parts that would receive the greatest degree of stress: at the joints, and as supports built into the torso itself.

After sizing, the whole surface was painted with water-based, flesh-colored tones and varnished. This thin finishing layer of clear varnish tended to discolor with age, giving many old composition dolls a faint yellowish cast. Attempts to wash off the varnish can damage the doll. The appearance of

BABY-WALKER DOLL (LEFT) *The all-composition construction of this c.1860s German doll extends even to its dress. The shoulder head is coated with a layer of wax. The doll's semi-mechanical movement allows its legs to move back and forth as the baby walker is wheeled along. Ht: 6in (15cm)*

KÄTHE KRUSE GIRL AND BOY (RIGHT) *These 1930s figures were designed by Käthe Kruse, a famous German maker who is usually associated with pressed felt dolls. Their composition socket heads were probably based on designs for cloth heads, made at an earlier period. Ht: 19in (48cm)*

Greiner and German Dolls

· 1840s to 1900s ·

ONE OF THE FOREMOST manufacturers of composition doll heads in the United States was Ludwig Greiner, based in Philadelphia. It was run by Greiner himself from 1840 to 1874. Thereafter, the company operated as Greiner Bros., in care of his sons, until 1883. Greiner was granted his first patent for a reinforced papier-mâché shoulder head in 1858. The patented recipe consisted of one pound each of pulped white paper, dry Spanish whiting, and rye flour; one ounce glue; and linen, which reinforced the heads. These were formed by pouring the mixture into plaster molds, and were then painted and varnished.

The large size of the heads dictated the use of correspondingly large bodies: most dolls with Greiner heads are over 13 inches in height. The stuffed bodies were either handmade by individuals, or were produced commercially by another company.

Early Greiner dolls bear a label on the back of the shoulder plate, marked "PATENT HEADS." Later models include the patent extension date, 1872.

Molded wavy hair has corkscrew curls at the back of the head and center parting

Head and shoulder plate cast as one unit and painted

Molded and painted facial features

Shoulder plate is glued onto the top of the torso

Well-defined closed mouth

Stuffed cloth upper arms, torso, and legs

Kid lower arms

Hands have separate, stitched fingers and thumbs

Seam at hipline allows doll to sit

"Seam" lines at knees formed by age and handling

Cotton lawn dress covers four layers of petticoats and pantaloons with eyelet lace trim

Damage to shoe reveals toes, formed by stitching

GREINER PATENT HEAD *This naked lady clearly demonstrates a convention that applies to most dolls: the head is disproportionately large for the size of the body parts. The reason for this is that the head is intended to embody and convey the doll's individual "personality."*

HT: 24in (60cm)

Open mouth shows bamboo teeth

FINE MASS-PRODUCED DOLL
(LEFT) Sonneberg, in Germany, produced many composition dolls for export. This 19th-century model has a wig, added over the usual painted hair of the papier-mâché shoulder head, and a gusseted kid body: both are signs of a good-quality product. Ht: 20in (50cm)

Gracefully modeled kid hands

Toes are stitched, but not separate

THE LOWER END OF THE MARKET
(RIGHT) This papier-mâché shoulder head was also made in Sonneberg in the 1820s–1830s. The stuffed cloth torso lacks shape, while the legs end in stubby feet, without toes. The arms are unjointed and made of kid. Ht: 26in (65cm)

Painted hair, with brushstroke "curls"; no wig

Kid arms are stitched to resemble gloves

Simply styled hair is molded and painted

Painted facial features

Papier-mâché shoulder head; molded and painted hair

Painted hazel eyes, with black pupils

Papier-mâché shoulder head, glued onto torso

Upper limbs and torso are tightly stuffed with sawdust

Closed mouth, painted red

Carved wooden lower arms and legs

Holes for sewing head onto cloth body

1840S PRE-GREINER DOLL
(BELOW) This doll closely resembles a Greiner, and it also has its origins in the United States. The papier-mâché shoulder head has molded and painted hair, which suggests a small boy's style; however, it could also serve as a girl's head. Ht: 40in (102cm)

Inset brown glass eyes; no pupils

Open/closed mouth with molded teeth

HOLZ-MASSE HEAD
(ABOVE) The German firm Cuno and Otto Dressel registered "Holz-Masse," meaning wood pulp, as a trademark in 1875. The mark was applied to heads of papier-mâché, composition, or wax-over-composition. This shoulder head, made c. 1890, is stamped with the symbol of a helmet with wings, which appeared as part of the original trademark. Ht: 6in (15cm)

Blue paper bands conceal joins; bands can also be red or green

LADY WITH PAINTED ORANGE SLIPPERS
(LEFT) Made in the 1830s, this doll is a typical Sonneberg export. The bands of blue paper at the elbows and knees cover and neaten the joins between the stuffed kid of the upper arms and legs and the carved wood of the lower limbs. Ht: 10in (25cm)

Real baby shoes, made of leather, date from 1869

Developments in Composition

· 1850s to 1930s ·

WHILE LENDING ITSELF ADMIRABLY to the construction of heads and large jointed bodies, composition proved to have two features that made it an unsatisfactory material for entire dolls: it was easily damaged, and its surface texture was subject to crazing, giving the dolls a worn appearance after only a short time. Yet some of the manufacturers found that composition had its advantages. Like bisque, it could be molded and painted – but unlike bisque, it did not need to be fired.

After 1900, many companies were established, predominantly in Germany and the United States, manufacturing a wide range of inexpensive all-composition dolls, as well as those with stuffed cloth or kid bodies. One such company was Stephan Schilling, which operated in the town of Sonneberg, in Germany, from 1878 to 1928.

Two lace-trimmed "tails," called lappets, at back of cap

Blond mohair wig, pinned in curls

Sleeping glass eyes, with heavily painted lashes and brows

Closed, painted mouth

Starched white cotton oversleeves

Composition shoulder head, glued onto torso

Stuffed cloth upper arms

Composition lower arms

Scissors and bone-handled penknife on silver-plated chatelaine

Spread-fingered hands; fingers and nails defined with red-painted lines

Back of the right thigh is stamped with Schilling's winged angel head trademark, registered in 1895

Stuffed cloth upper legs

Original period costume

Well-shaped composition lower legs

Toes are molded, but not separate

Dress conceals undergarments, including green-and-white striped corset with elastic garters and black stockings

C.1900 SCHILLING DOLL *The English nanny who gave this doll to her charge in 1904 dressed it in an exact replica of her own uniform. Although it is of good quality for its type, the relative cheapness of the doll is indicated by the body, which is straw-filled; more expensive dolls were stuffed with animal hair or other soft fibers.*

HT: 24in (60cm)

Tufts of woolen hair and earrings suggest "ethnic" appearance

Composition socket head

Composition bent arms

Accessories include a stork-shaped hanger, swan's-down powder puff, a bristle brush, mirror, and combs

DOLL IN CANE BASKET

(RIGHT) This 1930s German doll has a composition flange neck head, an open mouth showing two bottom teeth, and sleeping glass eyes with metal eyelids. Its stuffed stockinette torso and limbs are stitch-jointed at the shoulders and hips. Ht: 12in (30cm)

Composition bent legs

"TOPSY" (ABOVE) Black dolls representing babies and toddlers grew in popularity during the 1920s and 1930s. As this c.1935 American example shows, the heads were often cast from the same molds as those used for Caucasian dolls. Ht: 12in (30cm)

Ribbed silk skullcap, with yellow silk braid-and-tassel trim

Reverse socket head

Inset glass eyes; no pupils

"SUSAN" (BELOW) Versatile composition could be tinted to produce a range of colors: dolls designed to represent ethnic children usually had hair painted black and skin painted brown. No attempt has been made to modify this doll's Caucasian features. Ht: 18in (46cm)

C.1855 TODDLER DOLL (RIGHT)

Made in Sonneberg, Germany, this black doll has realistic, molded, non-Caucasian features. A bellows squeaker is housed within the torso of its fully jointed, papier-mâché, Mottschmann-type body. Ht: 8in (20cm)

Shiny light brown glaze indicates that this is a good-quality doll

All-composition construction, jointed at shoulders and hips, with bent limbs

Composition head, with sleeping, flirty glass eyes

The mark on the back of the neck clearly identifies this model.

Gown conceals stuffed cloth torso

Lower legs are jointed at ankles

Unjointed bent limbs made of composition

SINGER SEWING MACHINE DOLL

(LEFT) This doll and its clothing, which shows examples of machine stitching, were used as a window display in one of Singer's London stores during World War II. It was made in the late 1930s by Seyfarth and Reinhardt of Germany, which operated from 1922 into the 1930s. Ht: 18in (46cm)

Original organdy dress

Long gown, coat, and bonnet are decorated with machine-quilting

Alexander Doll Company
· 1926 to the present day ·

IN 1926, SISTERS ROSE AND BERTHA ALEXANDER (who later changed her name to Beatrice) founded the Alexander Doll Company of New York. This firm is known even today for its quality products. Many of its early dolls were inspired by living or fictional characters, such as Shirley Temple or the glamorous heroine of *Gone With The Wind*, Scarlett O'Hara. On May 28, 1934, five little girls were born to the Dionne family just outside Montreal, in Canada. These babies quickly became media personalities, and many doll manufacturers grasped the marketing opportunity presented by such a novel event. However, only the Alexander Doll Co. was granted the right to register the Dionne Quintuplets as a trademark in 1936 in the United States. This set of dolls formed part of the firm's highly collectible Madame Alexander line.

Molded and painted hair

Sleeping brown eyes

Composition doll, jointed with elastic stringing at neck, shoulders, and hips

Human hair upper lashes; painted lower lashes and brows

Open/closed painted mouth

Arms are bent, but straighter than those of the babies

Chubby torso and limbs

Straight legs allow doll to stand unaided

Flat feet, with dimpled toes

Green trimmings are exclusive to Cecile

Doll's name is engraved on a medal pinned to its dress

White cotton socks

Cloth ankle-strap shoes, with metal buckles on toes and snap fastenings

DIONNE TODDLER DOLLS *In 1937, two years after the creation of the baby dolls, the Dionne toddlers were produced so that the line kept pace with the development of the real-life quints. All five dolls are identical, and are distinguished only by the different colors of clothes and accessories: Annette wears yellow; Marie, blue; Yvonne, pink; Cecile, green; and Emelie, lavender.*

HT: 11½in (29cm)

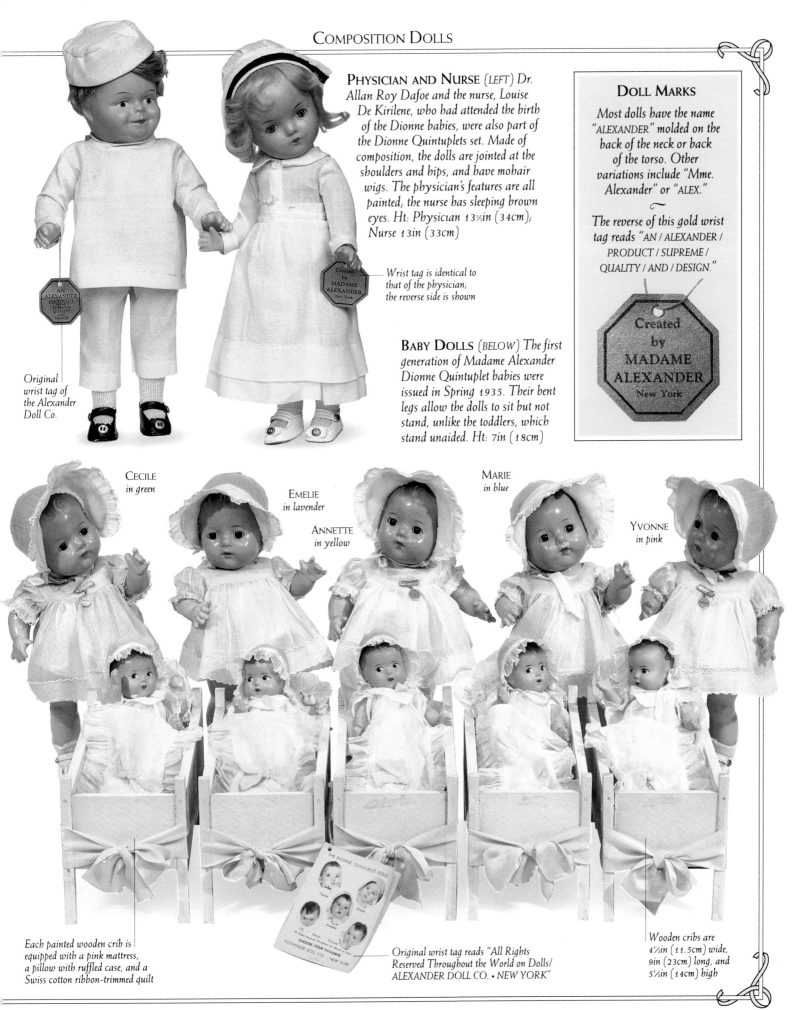

PHYSICIAN AND NURSE (LEFT) Dr.
Allan Roy Dafoe and the nurse, Louise
De Kirilene, who had attended the birth
of the Dionne babies, were also part of
the Dionne Quintuplets set. Made of
composition, the dolls are jointed at the
shoulders and hips, and have mohair
wigs. The physician's features are all
painted; the nurse has sleeping brown
eyes. Ht: Physician 13½in (34cm);
Nurse 13in (33cm)

Wrist tag is identical to
that of the physician;
the reverse side is shown

DOLL MARKS

Most dolls have the name
"ALEXANDER" molded on the
back of the neck or back
of the torso. Other
variations include "Mme.
Alexander" or "ALEX."

The reverse of this gold wrist
tag reads "AN / ALEXANDER /
PRODUCT / SUPREME /
QUALITY / AND / DESIGN."

Created
by
MADAME
ALEXANDER
New York

BABY DOLLS (BELOW) The first
generation of Madame Alexander
Dionne Quintuplet babies were
issued in Spring 1935. Their bent
legs allow the dolls to sit but not
stand, unlike the toddlers, which
stand unaided. Ht: 7in (18cm)

Original
wrist tag of
the Alexander
Doll Co.

CECILE
in green

EMELIE
in lavender

ANNETTE
in yellow

MARIE
in blue

YVONNE
in pink

Each painted wooden crib is
equipped with a pink mattress,
a pillow with ruffled case, and a
Swiss cotton ribbon-trimmed quilt

Original wrist tag reads "All Rights
Reserved Throughout the World on Dolls/
ALEXANDER DOLL CO. • NEW YORK"

Wooden cribs are
4½in (11.5cm) wide,
9in (23cm) long, and
5½in (14cm) high

Wax-over-composition Dolls

· 1830s to 1900s ·

THE IDEA OF ENHANCING composition with wax was realized by many German doll-head makers starting in c.1830. Between 1870 and 1900, a small number of English companies in London also manufactured wax-over-composition heads; these were attached to stuffed cloth bodies. The English dolls are usually very well marked with body stamps; if there are no markings, wax-over-composition dolls are usually assumed to be of German origin.

⌁ The manufacturing process involved applying a thin layer of wax over heads, and also limbs, made of composition, to give the surface a smoother and more natural appearance. Wax-over-composition dolls looked better than those made of composition alone; they also had the advantage of being significantly cheaper – both to manufacture and to buy – than their poured wax relatives (see pages 30–41).

Silk-lined velvet hat is tied with lace-trimmed organdy ribbons and secured with blue glass-headed hatpins

Curled auburn mohair wig

Inset blue-gray glass eyes

Molded and painted mouth shows two rows of small teeth

Cape is made of silk and poplin

Finely modeled shoulder head has a thin tinted layer of wax over its composition base

Wax-over-composition arms

Starched cotton apron over a button-fronted cotton bodice and skirt

Glazed cotton upper legs and torso are stuffed with straw

Composition lower legs

Feet are molded and painted to show stylish side-buttoning boots with heels

C.1900 GERMAN DOLL

The young owner who dubbed this pretty lady "Nurse Cross" could hardly have chosen a less apt name, for the doll's half-smiling expression radiates anything but displeasure. The costume is a detailed replica of the uniform worn by a child's nanny in England c.1900.

HT: 17in (43cm)

Penny toy bought from street vendor on Ludgate Hill, London

C.1830 BAGMAN'S BABY (LEFT)
Cheap German-made dolls were once
a common item of merchandise for
peddlers, often referred to in England
at the time as "Bagmen." The
method of inserting the wig into the
head through a vertical groove cut
in the crown also gives these dolls the
name of "slit-head." Ht: 27in (68cm)

Shoulder
head is made
of plaster

Pink kid arms,
separate fingers
and thumbs

Dress conceals
stuffed cloth
torso and legs

Beneath dress, a wire
protruding through the base
of the lower torso opens and
closes the glass eyes

Elaborate, felt-topped headdress, made of black animal
fur and secured with a "gold"
chain chinstrap

Auburn
mohair wig

Open mouth
shows three teeth

Sleeves hide unjointed
composition arms

Hands have separate
thumbs and joined
fingers, delineated
with painted red lines

Costume conceals hard,
stuffed cloth upper legs
and torso, stitched at hips

Handmade
Highland
Regimental
costume

**SCOTTISH COSTUME
DOLL** (LEFT) Typical of
dolls produced in Germany
and exported throughout
Europe, this finely dressed
1890s model has a wax-
over-composition shoulder
head, and unjointed arms and
lower legs of composition. The inset
blue glass eyes have light irises and
darker pupils, and are an advance
on the pupilless eyes of many earlier
models. Ht: 14in (35cm)

**C.1860 GERMAN DOLL
WITH ALICE BAND** (RIGHT)
Fashionable hairstyles, sometimes
accessorized, as shown in this
example, were molded with
the head and painted before
the application of the wax
coating. Dolls with molded
and painted hair tended to be
less expensive than those
with either human hair
or mohair wigs.
Ht: 18in (46cm)

Lead-weighted
sleeping eyes,
with metal
eyelids

Dress conceals
body, made
in the 1850s,
which predates
the doll's
C.1860s
head

Wooden lower legs, painted
to show flat-heeled boots

LATE 19TH-CENTURY GIRL
(RIGHT) Thick wax covers the
composition of this German shoulder
head, and a lead-weight mechanism
operates the sleeping glass eyes.
The hands are well modeled, yet
the maker has not cleaned up the
casting lines at the ends of the
fingers. Ht: 17½in (45cm)

Wooden lower
arms with spoon-
shaped hands

Ash blond
mohair wig

Printed cotton
dress is older
than the doll

Composition
lower arms
and legs

Poured Wax Dolls

One of the original uses for wax was for making religious effigies and votive offerings. This practice, widespread in Roman Catholic parts of Europe, gave many makers their first experience in wax modeling. Seeking new expression for their creativity, these craftsmen carried their skills to London, where, by the nineteenth century, they had established an unrivaled tradition of wax doll-making.

SOME OF THE MOST inspired European doll-makers worked in England between 1850 and 1930. Their originality was matched by their choice of material: translucent, luminous, and warm to the touch, wax is perfectly suited to creating dolls, in particular portrait dolls, which rely on the faithful reproduction of facial features and skin tones for their realism.

Casting the Head

The nineteenth-century wax modelers all followed the same technical, yet simple, process to create their doll heads. The first stage involved the skilled modeling of the head in wax or clay. From this, a cast was produced in the form of a two- or three-part plaster mold. The molten wax mixture, a blend of coloring, bleached beeswax, and a number of other additives, was poured into the mold. It was allowed only a brief time to set

before the excess mixture was poured out. Some heads were made with a single pouring; others were built up using multiple layers of wax, a method which produced a stronger head with a more translucent, skinlike texture. In either case, the final thickness of the wax was no more than ⅛in (3mm). After the wax had cooled and solidified, the casting was lifted from the mold, and any traces of the casting lines were removed from the sides of the head.

It was the finishing processes that determined whether or not the head was a good one. Blown or molded glass eyes, set into the cut-out and shaped eye sockets, were fixed with either a small extra amount of wax, or warming the socket to melt the surrounding wax. Sleeping eyes are rarely found in poured wax heads, but when used were normally on a push–pull wire. The standard type of lead-weight mechanism can cause damage inside the head if it knocks about. The doll's hair was applied next,

1806 ENGLISH DOLL (*LEFT*) *This small, beady-eyed figure shows the special feature of early dolls: a shoulder head and lower limbs molded entirely from solid wax. Its feet have been cast and dipped in green-colored wax to resemble shoes. The torso and upper limbs are made of stuffed cloth. Ht: 6in (13cm)*

PLASTER MOLD (*RIGHT*) *Cast wax doll heads are always hollow, and made in a mold of three or, as seen here, two parts. The two lugs at the top fit snugly into correspondingly positioned holes on the other half of the mold, which forms the back of the head.*

THE MANUFACTURE OF GERMAN WAX DOLLS (LEFT)
This engraving, reproduced in the November 26, 1887, edition of The Queen, The Lady's Newspaper, illustrates the following eight steps, showing how a wax-headed doll was created and finished: 1. Making the Model; 2. Joining the Head; 3. Setting the Eyes; 4. Waxing the Head; 5. Painting the Face; 6. Dressing the Hair; 7. Fixing the Head; 8. Dressing the Finished Doll.

MONTANARI MARK (ABOVE)
Wax heads are rarely signed, but their cloth bodies may carry the maker's name. Mme. Montanari's handwritten signatures sometimes include her business address, as here.

inserted as either single strands or as small clumps into fine cuts or pinholes in the head. (Hair eyelashes were similarly inset.) This way, the hair seems to grow from the scalp; it has more natural movement than can be achieved with a wig; and it enhances the realistic appearance of the head itself. Both human hair and mohair were used; sometimes the two were combined on the same head. Buyers could even have snippings of their own child's hair inset at almost no additional cost. Finally, coloring was applied to the mouth and the whole surface was dusted with fine pumice to remove the shine.

Completing the Doll

Poured wax heads usually have deep shoulder plates. The head is sewn to the body through a hole at each of the lower corners of the front and back plates. In better quality dolls, grommets or metal eyelets reinforce the holes and protect them from wear and tear. The cloth bodies, usually rather lumpy in shape, are made of calico. They are stuffed with cow or other animal hair, or woolly fibers, but rarely sawdust. To ensure an exact color match, heads and limbs for complete sets of dolls were produced during the same casting session. Most poured wax arms were cast to above the elbow joint, and legs to above the knee. These, too, had grommets embedded in the wax, and were attached to the upper stuffed cloth limbs the same way as the head was to the torso.

In what was still largely a home-based business, each one of these steps in the finishing process was assigned to a particular member of the family. Enduring very poor conditions, and dealing with dangerous materials, many of the workers paid a high price for their occupation. Molten wax, which was poured at extremely high temperatures, often caused severe burns; the materials with which the bodies were stuffed contained tiny particles of dust that, if inhaled, could lead to breathing difficulties; but perhaps the most hazardous of all was the white lead used to color the wax, which proved to be an insidious – and in some instances deadly – poison.

1980s PORTRAIT DOLL
(RIGHT) This is doll number 4001 in a limited-edition series of 5,000 portrait dolls that represent Peggy Nisbet. The dolls were designed by the House of Nisbet in consultation with Faith Eaton – an English doll authority – to commemorate the company's founder. Ht: 18in (46cm)

Early Dolls

· 1750s to 1850s ·

THE MAJORITY OF WAX-HEADED DOLLS that have survived date from the past two centuries. Even the earliest of these dolls show the skill of the wax modeler. Most were expensive to buy, so it is quite unlikely that they were ever treated as throw-away items. The fact that only a few were made is a more satisfactory explanation for their relative scarcity now, than questions of quality.

⁓ Many wax dolls appear to be almost exact copies of each other. However, their similarity merely reflects contemporary fashion and style, as with modern-day favorites like Barbie or G.I. Joe. For example, wax doll heads created between 1750 and 1850 are modeled to show a high forehead. In Georgian England, this was a visible sign of good breeding and refined sensibility.

⁓ Inset glass eyes, another common feature, are pupilless and black in pre-1820s dolls. By the 1830s, makers could choose colored eyes, which were usually blue glass with black pupils, to give their dolls a more realistic expression.

Wax shoulder head, with inset pupilless black glass eyes

Molded and painted facial features

Satin stole is a later addition

Painted brownish black curly hair shows a typical style of the period

Sleeves conceal stuffed-cloth upper arms

Lower arms to above elbow joint are made of wax

Ears are simple shapes, set close to the sides of the head

Dress conceals stuffed upper legs and torso, made of striped mattress ticking

Shoulder plate is very deep

Off-white, very fine cotton muslin dress, with petticoat and bloomers beneath

1812 HEIRLOOM DOLL, "BESSIE"

The essence of any doll is conveyed in its head, and this fine example of early wax modeling suggests an accomplished maker. Lovely "Bessie" was the homecoming gift of Captain Nathaniel Osgood — a young shipmaster living in the Atlantic seaboard town of Salem, Massachusetts — to his small daughter, Elizabeth.

HT: 20in (50cm)

Inset auburn human hair

Wax head to base of neck; upper torso made of calico painted in flesh tones

Upper arms, torso, and legs are made of stuffed calico

Wax lower arms

Beneath the dress, doll wears a complete set of linen undergarments

Wooden cradle decorated with Regency-patterned paper and bead finials

Inset mohair and painted facial features on all three dolls

Red-painted shoes are hollow and very fragile

SHADOWBOX TRIO (ABOVE) All-wax, hollow dolls are usually quite small, because of their fragility. Made in England and Germany from 1790 to 1820, they were popular ornaments, and were often displayed in a glass-fronted case. Ht: 1½–2½in (4–6cm)

1758 COSTUME DOLL (ABOVE) Young English lady Laetitia Clark designed and made this splendid silk outfit, which she called "A Long Robe Coat Dress for a Lady of Sixteen." The doll itself is nicely modeled, but owes its fame entirely to its clothes and their maker. Ht: 13in (33cm)

Pale wax shoulder head

Dress conceals stuffed calico upper arms, torso, and legs

Wax shoulder head

Poured wax lower arms to above elbow joint

Inset bright blue glass eyes, with pupils

Dress conceals stuffed cloth legs and torso stitched at hips

Red molded wax shoes

1757 "PARTY DRESS" DOLL (ABOVE) This simple costume was also designed and sewn by Laetitia Clark (see top left). Red was widely used for doll footwear at this period. By the end of the 1790s, green was the favored color. Ht: 8in (20cm)

TWIN SISTERS (LEFT) Made in England c.1838 and representing twins, these dolls are identical — something of a rarity — down to their lace-trimmed pantalettes. The fading of the shoulder heads to pale beige is due to natural changes in the wax. Ht: 20in (50cm)

Hand-stitched leather shoes

Original, fine cotton clothing

English Makers

· 1850s to 1930s ·

TOWARD THE MIDDLE of the nineteenth century, wax became an increasingly popular material for creating doll heads and limbs. By far the greatest exponents of the craft were the English-born and émigré, often Italian, makers who were based in London. During the next 50 years, wax doll-making reached its zenith, particularly with the achievements of such virtuosi as the Pierottis (see pages 36–39) and Montanaris. Examples of their work were displayed and won prizes at international exhibitions.

The Great Exhibition of 1851, held at the Crystal Palace in London's Hyde Park, helped to establish the reputations of many makers. Madame Augusta Montanari won her first medal at this event. A great number of her dolls were portraits, some of which represented Queen Victoria's children. Perhaps it was this, rather than the medal she won, that earned her the patronage of the queen.

Quilted and ruched silk bonnet, tied with satin ribbons

Blond hair is set into the head in small clumps

Three-tiered carrying cape

Blue glass eyes, set into sockets

Two grommets, for sewing head to torso

Lavish silk tassel and braid trimming

Poured wax lower arms, cast to include the elbow joints

Chubby baby hands and wrists

Hip seams attach legs to stuffed calico torso and allow doll to sit

Legs can bend at seamed knees

Poured wax lower legs; feet have well-defined toes showing toe-nails

HT: 26in (65cm)

MONTANARI DOLL

A usual practice among makers of this time was to team baby heads and limbs with adult bodies. True baby-doll bodies had shapeless torsos, but because the body was intended to be covered up, its form scarcely mattered. This 1870s Montanari baby doll is dressed in period Edwardian clothing.

Long lawn robe was everyday late 19th-century baby attire

Inset human hair

Wax shoulder head, colored in pink tones

Sleeves cover stuffed calico upper arms

Very full head of inset human hair

Meech's southeast London workshop address is stamped on the doll's thigh.

Wire-operated, sleeping brown glass eyes

LUCY PECK HEAD (ABOVE)
A high proportion of beeswax used in the casting gives this c.1900 *shoulder head its dark flesh tone. Ht: 27in (68cm)*

Dress conceals stuffed calico upper legs and torso

BY ROYAL APPOINTMENT
(ABOVE) *This 1883 shoulder head shows the talent of Londoner Herbert John Meech, who worked between 1865 and 1917. Royal patronage entitled him to use the crest that he included with many of his body stamps. Ht: 23in (58cm)*

Inset auburn human hair

Wax shoulder head; modeled facial features represent those of a young girl

Wood-handled silk parasol opens and closes

Lower arms to above elbow are made of wax

"C. C." incised on the sole is the mark of an unidentified maker

LUCY PECK GIRL (ABOVE) *From 1891 to 1930, Lucy Peck made dolls and ran a repair service. She designed and created this 1890s example, but the dolls she repaired would often also bear her firm's mark. Ht: 20in (50cm)*

The ink stamp appears on the back of the doll's torso.

1880S SOHO BAZAAR DOLL
(RIGHT) *Charles Marsh came from a famous family of doll-makers and repairers, and worked between 1878 and 1895. His dolls are wax-over-composition, wax-over-papier-mâché, or poured wax, as here. Ht: 18in (46cm)*

The stamp on the doll's torso clearly identifies the maker.

Human hair from the future owner was often inset into the doll's head

Inset glass eyes; human hair lashes and brows

Pale wax lower legs and arms

The Pierotti Family

· 1770s to 1935 ·

THE PIEROTTIS WERE NOT SIMPLY doll-makers. They were (and called themselves) wax modelers. The company was established by Domenico Pierotti, an Italian who married an English girl and learned the essential skills of plaster mold-making as well as wax casting and modeling from her family. One of their 12 children, Anerico Cephas, born 1809, carried the wax-modeling business forward and perfected the poured wax method for the production of heads. His son, Charles William, was also an innovative wax modeler. Many of the designs created by these two were adapted by later members of the family. In 1935, with the retirement of Charles Ernest, Charles William's son, four generations of family business came to an end.

Straw boater is contemporary, but not original to doll

Inset violet-blue glass eyes

Clothing belonged to a real child and dates from 1872

Long titian mohair inserted into the wax

Eyebrows and lashes of mohair match that of hair

Stuffed cloth upper arms are sewn to torso under the shoulder plate

Threads, waxed with resin, attach the shoulder head to the torso

Upper legs, made separately from the torso, attached with seams at hips

Calico torso, stuffed with cowhair

Lower limbs are secured to upper limbs by thread through the grommets

Lower legs have shaped calves, and feet showing insteps

Hands have dimpled knuckles and short, stubby fingers

Hem of dress is decorated with pattern of trailing vine leaves

Socks and shoes are made of silk

HENRY PIEROTTI, GIRL *Anerico Cephas Pierotti is usually known by the anglicized name Henry. This doll, which he made c.1870, represents a young girl. Its wax shoulder head and lower limbs are colored peach, rather than the standard pink. The doll's straw boater, cotton dress, and silk socks and shoes belonged to a child, and date from 1872.*

HT: 24in (60cm)

1920S FORTUNE TELLER

(LEFT) Charles Ernest Pierotti made this unique doll to raise money at a Masonic bazaar. It has a legless body fitted onto a wooden stick handle. As the stick was twirled, streamers with fortunes flew out, like the ribbons of a maypole. The shoulder head and limbs are made of darkly colored wax, which gives the doll an exotic and gypsylike appearance. Ht: 27in (68cm)

Inset brown glass eyes

Black hair is a combination of inset human hair and mohair

Costume, made by Eleanor Bessie Pierotti, cannot be removed

Hands have slender, delicate fingers and thumbs

Gracefully modeled wax lower arms

Skirt would have had cloth and paper streamers attached to the waistband

Wooden stick is joined to doll's stuffed cloth torso

Head made of thin, single layer of wax

Portrait head of an unknown old man

Portrait head of young woman; finished portrait heads were discarded if not true likenesses

Blown glass eyes are rounded and bulbous

Blue, gray, or brown eyes were used for portrait dolls, depending on color of person's eyes

Molded glass eyes are lozenge-shaped

Crown is set with "pearls" and encrusted with colored glass "gems"

Inset blue glass eyes, with pupils

Blue velvet Cap of Estate, inside the crown, is edged with miniver

Inset human hair, braided and coiled around head

Pale wax shoulder head

Fur tippet is draped over top of cloak

Darker wax arms, cast to above elbow joint

Fur-trimmed velvet cloak covers the naked back of the doll

Crown shows "scar" where head was cut to insert eyes and then repaired

Silk and net, sequined gown extends only to doll's sides

Titian mohair, wound around sticks, is curled into ringlets

Wooden sticks, joined with strips of linen gauze

C.1840 QUEEN VICTORIA

(ABOVE) Henry Pierotti was an especially gifted wax modeler, and created many of the portrait dolls for which the family became famous. The strong resemblance of this model to the young queen is a testament to his ability. Ht: 19in (48cm)

PROTOTYPES AND PARTS

(LEFT) Experiments formed a vital element of the Pierottis' work, and not all resulted in viable products. Prototype heads, like these of an old man and a young woman, were made of a single layer of very thin and fragile wax. The eyes and hair were particularly important features, helping to give the dolls expression and personality.

Pierotti Portrait Dolls

· 1900s to 1930s ·

WAX MODELERS were quick to discover that the material offered unique possibilities for rendering highly realistic portrait heads. Members of royal families, soldiers, and statesmen were all popular subjects. Henry Pierotti was one of a few wax portrait modelers who created dolls representing Queen Victoria (see page 37) and Lord Roberts (see below). Other dolls have no known sitter, but are clearly portraits – perhaps of friends or family – to judge by their idiosyncratic facial features and expressions.

～ Carrying the realism further, the Pierottis introduced three styles of body that corresponded to the age and gender of the person the doll was to represent. The standard shape – chubby shoulders, a narrow waist, and broad hips – was used for most of the dolls, except those portraying babies and men.

White mohair, inset to show a receding hairline

Blown glass eyes with mohair brows and upper lashes

Mohair mustache and goatee

Brownish patina often forms as the wax ages

Long, stuffed cloth arms; typical feature of male dolls

Full dress uniform, decorated with gold braid, brass buttons, ceremonial medals, and rank insignia

Shoulder head is secured to torso by thread through grommets

Large poured wax hands, cast to above wrist joint; typical feature of male dolls

Sleeve slash and stripe denote rank of Commander-in-Chief

Hamley Bros. tag: the Regent Street, London, toyshop was formerly located at 812 Oxford Street

Lower half of stuffed cloth torso extends to form the upper legs; typical feature of male dolls

Poured wax lower legs; only one style was made

White kid breeches

Black leather gaiters and black leather shoes, made to represent boots

Sword, sheathed in a leather scabbard

HT: 20in (50cm)

LORD ROBERTS AND MALE DOLL BODY

This tribute to Lord Roberts – Commander-in-Chief of the British Army during the Boer War – was modeled by Charles Ernest Pierotti c.1900, adapted from an earlier model created by Charles William Pierotti. The naked doll shows the characteristics of the male body style.

STANDARD BABY HEAD

(RIGHT) Pierotti nonportrait baby dolls have one style of head. The eyes are of inset blue glass, with blond mohair lashes and brows; the hair is also inset blond mohair. A delicate pursing of the lips gives the mouth a bowed, slightly open shape. Ht: 20in (50cm)

Mohair is set into the head in small clumps

Childlike nose, with broad bridge

Molded, closed mouth, painted red

Shoulder head has a short, thick neck and plump chest

C.1900 PORTRAIT BABY HEAD

(LEFT) Charles Ernest Pierotti produced this portrait of his only child, Patrick Enrico, who died when still very young. The fragile beauty of the infant is evident in the subtle pink coloring of the wax, the large pale blue glass eyes, and the gold-blond mohair curled over the forehead and around the sides of the face. Ht: 22in (55cm)

Lace-trimmed silk robe, adorned with cream satin ribbons and French knots

Inset mohair or human hair

Standard poured wax baby shoulder head

Blue eyes were usual; buyers could choose other colors

No grommets in sew holes on cheaper models

Joined fingers and separate thumbs

Small feet are in proportion to the hands

Inset blue glass eyes, with painted facial features

Well-defined chin and jawline

Inset long strawberry-blond mohair, caught up at back of head into a loose braid

Pale wax shoulder head has a slim neck

Elaborate leg-o'-mutton dress sleeves, with stitched knife-pleating

Fingerless lace mittens have half-thumbs

HEAD PROFILE (ABOVE)

The elegant curves of this young woman's head and shoulders contrast with the chubby, fleshy modeling of the neck and shoulders of the Pierotti baby dolls.

COSTUME DISPLAY DOLL

(RIGHT) In the early 20th century, fashionable London shops and dress designers enticed would-be clients with miniature versions of their latest creations, exhibited on doll models. This c.1910 portrait of a young lady displays an off-the-shoulder striped silk taffeta evening gown. The fine shoulder head is teamed with the narrow-waisted, stuffed cloth body that was used for all dolls except babies and men. Ht: 16in (40cm)

C.1905 BABY DOLL (ABOVE)

The stuffed calico or glazed cotton torso of the stylized baby body is waistless, and usually extends to the upper legs, unless the doll is large. The upper arms, of the same fabric, are sewn to the torso under the shoulder plate. The poured wax lower arms are cast to above the bent elbow joint. Ht: 12in (30cm)

"Princess Daisy"

· 1890s ·

SEEN IN THE LIGHT of their quirky history, some otherwise rather unremarkable dolls can acquire great charm. In 1894, when Miss Twiss, living in Amsterdam, Holland, purchased a rather plain English wax doll, the city was preparing to host the International Exposition that was to be held the following year. Miss Twiss had the idea of commissioning Dutch craftsmen to make clothes and accessories for the doll, which would be used as a model to display their work at the exposition.

The display was purchased by a group of English ladies, who presented the doll, "Princess Daisy," and her extensive trousseau to Princess Mary of Teck (who was later queen to George V, King of England) as a christening gift for her daughter Mary, born in 1897.

Inset very pale blond mohair

Poured wax shoulder head

Rosettes and streamers, attached to waist ribbon, match those on the bonnet

Sleeping blue glass eyes; mohair eyebrows and upper lashes

Wide band of cream moiré silk ribbon, tied in a bow, secures the doll to its cushion

Poured wax lower arms, cast to above elbow joint

Stuffed calico upper limbs and torso

Buttoned, padded drawers, worn over diapers

Darker bands of calico cover the joins

Poured wax lower legs, cast to above knee joint

Muslin christening robe, inset with broderie anglaise

HT: 18in (46cm)

CEREMONIAL PRESENTATION *"Princess Daisy" is displayed lying on her own christening cushion, as was the custom in late 19th-century England when babies were presented for baptism. The cotton lawn cushion is padded with eiderdown and has a slipcover of silk-embroidered, lace-edged muslin. The doll wears a lace bonnet, trimmed with silk ribbon rosettes, and a traditional christening robe over a satin underdress and linen undergarments.*

Handmade brass clothes stands are part of the doll's accessories

Decorative pink satin bows on shoulders of dress

Pink ribbon sash matches the satin bows on the shoulders

Afternoon dress, made of cotton lawn and embroidered with daisies

Large satin bows and rosettes decorate almost every item

Satin traveling cloak, with lace-trimmed cape and elaborate lace collar

ROYAL APPAREL (LEFT) Miss

Twiss provided an inventory, listing each piece of clothing in "Princess Daisy's" wardrobe. Every item uses only the finest natural materials — muslin, silk, satin, and wool — and is embroidered with either the initial "D" or the doll's name, "Daisy," depending on its size.

CANOPIED CRADLE (BELOW)

The specially commissioned accessories include a wrought-iron stand with curlicued stretchers and legs, which allows the metal cradle to swing gently to and fro; six top and bottom sheets, pillowcases, and blankets; and an ivory cross with winged cherub, to ensure "Princess Daisy" sweet dreams.

Two-layered canopy, made of Swiss dot cotton over satin

Padded satin quilt

LAYETTE BASKET AND CHRISTENING GIFTS (BELOW)

The satin-lined basket contains myriad accessories, including a real sponge in an oiled silk bag, tiny safety pins, soaps, and a silver bed-warmer. Only the rubber nipples for the baby bottles and the box of special cookies have perished with time.

Satin and lace bonnet hangs on its own brass hat stand

Wooden sock hangers

Basket stands on four plaited wicker feet

Hallmarked silver spoons and fork

Real gold "Daisy" name pin and bracelet

Real pearl necklace, with a pavé diamond clasp

Forged iron cradle and stand, painted white, with gold paint edging and trim

Porcelain Dolls

One of the most fascinating aspects of language is that individual words – which have precise definitions – can take on a variety of imprecise connotations in everyday speech. The word "porcelain," for example, seems to acquire different meanings when used by different people. As a term in our special doll language, however, porcelain describes with a single word three types of doll head: glazed china; untinted bisque; and bisque.

THE PRODUCTION OF porcelain doll heads was rarely the principal output of any manufacturer, so it is useful to understand the development of porcelain as a doll-making material in its historical context. This very fine grade of ceramicware is fired in a kiln at not less than 2,372°F (1,300°C). Few clays are able to withstand such extreme temperatures: feldspathic china clay, or kaolin, and china stone are two that can.

〜 The discovery of these clays in parts of Germany at the beginning of the eighteenth century led to the establishment of the Meissen factory, near Dresden, in 1709. In Cornwall, in southwestern England, clay-pits revealed sufficient reserves for the first manufacture of porcelain items in 1770. Extensive deposits of these naturally occurring clays were mined throughout Germany, especially in the region of Thuringia. The porcelain industry flourished there, with a number of factories churning out inexpensive

figurines and decorative ornaments, as well as the exquisite domestic tableware that was their stock in trade. For many manufacturers, the production of doll heads was nothing more than a lucrative sideline.

Moldings and Castings

After the start of the nineteenth century, porcelain began to enjoy increasing favor with the doll-head manufacturers. This popularity lasted for the next hundred years or so, when porcelain was supplanted by the new, more versatile compositions and plastics introduced in the first quarter of the twentieth century. All the porcelain doll heads that were manufactured in

GLAZED CHINA DOLLS (LEFT) *In the United States, all three of these dolls are called Frozen Charlottes. In Britain, the larger figures are known as Bath Dolls. At Christmas, the smaller ones were often hidden inside plum puddings as good-luck charms, earning them the name Pudding Dolls. Ht: Largest 18in (46cm); smallest 1in (2.5cm)*

UNTINTED BISQUE SHOULDER HEAD (RIGHT) *Dolls made in the late 1860s classical style owe much to the ideas of ancient Greece and Rome. The typical formality of the style, shown in the modeling of this German doll's head, is echoed in the Greek key pattern that decorates its pretty cotton dress. Ht: 16in (40cm)* the nineteenth century were produced in molds. Like those used in poured wax castings (see pages 30–31), these were made of plaster and in two or three parts. In the early days, a porcelain mixture with a malleable, doughlike consistency was pressed into the molds for shaping. Refining their production techniques, manufacturers introduced a wetter fluid mixture that could be poured rather than pressed into the molds.

Glazing and Finishing

The heads were usually given three separate firings and two layers of glaze. The initial firing produced biscuitware, or bisque, so called because of its close, brittle texture. The second and third firings fused the painted decorations and glazes. After the firings, the appearance of the heads identifies each of the three different types: glazed china heads are those with a shiny overglaze; untinted bisque heads have a matte finish and are usually white; bisque heads are tinted with a tinge of color. Manufacturers produced both shoulder and socket heads, and achieved equally good results with pressed and poured porcelain. From the outside, pressed heads cannot be distinguished from poured ones and give no clue to the casting method

C.1860 GLAZED CHINA HEAD

"THE DAY BEFORE MARRIAGE" c.1838 George Baxter aquatint

C.1850 GLAZED CHINA HEAD

C.1840 GLAZED CHINA HEAD

GLAZED CHINA SHOULDER HEAD (LEFT) *Similarities between this doll and the untinted bisque lady at far left are no coincidence, as both were made in Germany* c.1865. *Likenesses include the hairstyles and facial features; pierced ears; the shoulder plate, which displays a molded blouse with a bow; and the stuffed cloth body with kid arms. Ht: 21in (53cm)*

LIFE RE-CREATED AS ART (ABOVE) *Wonderfully detailed hairstyles, molded and painted as braided buns, ringlets, curls, or even done up in net snoods, are the special feature of porcelain doll heads. The young lady depicted in the aquatint "The Day Before Marriage" (top right) shows how faithfully these styles were modeled on real people. The three glazed china heads (above) are described on page 45.*

used. However, there are some differences that can be seen from examination of the inside of the head. A pressed head is likely to be found to have a rough inner surface and will be uneven in thickness; the insides of poured heads, on the other hand, are smooth and consistently even.

∽ The fine texture of porcelain allowed the delicate molding of much ornamental detail. Many porcelain doll heads were cast to show the fashionable hairstyles of the period, and these usually also have molded and painted eyes. Other heads were left plain: the crown was cut away so that glass eyes could be inserted, and a wig was attached as part of the finishing process.

∽ Molded hairstyles were largely replaced by hair wigs after 1870, as they were considered to be more natural. The introduction of porcelain character dolls in the early twentieth century saw a revival in molded and painted hair, but the extremely decorative styles of the mid-nineteenth century were never repeated.

Fancy Glazed China Heads

· 1830s to 1880s ·

WHEN GERMAN MAKERS introduced the first porcelain doll heads with molded hairstyles in the 1830s, a variety of quality dolls came onto the market. These early shoulder heads are called glazed chinas because they are overglazed – a finish that makes them glossy while retaining the whiteness of the porcelain. The coloring of the cheeks and facial features is fixed in the underglaze, but it is quite rare for such heads to be tinted overall with flesh tones.

Reflecting real-life trends, the styling and adornment of the dolls' hair closely followed contemporary fashions. The clothing that was designed for the finished glazed china dolls was equally modish, and usually shows the most up-to-the-minute outfits as worn by the young ladies of the period.

Hair is styled with a center parting that has been left white

Molded side bows, with touches of gold paint, are a special feature

Hair is held in a snood at the back of the head

Eyebrows and upper lids are finely detailed in black paint

Shoulder head is sewn to body through holes in front and back of shoulder plate

Stitched seams form joints at shoulders

Overlarge hands: this body type was used to teach girls about human anatomy

Stuffed cloth arms

Torso is hand-seamed at the left side

Stitched seams at knees and hips allow limited movement

Cotton skirt and bodice, with frilled peplum at waist

Feet have no toes

C.1865 GERMAN DOLL WITH MARY HEAD *In the 1860s, wearing gilded hair bows was such a popular style with Mary Todd Lincoln – wife of President Abraham Lincoln – that doll heads showing her favorite coiffure are often named after her.*

HT: 23in (58cm)

C.1840 GERMAN HEAD
(LEFT) The high quality of this shoulder head is indicated by the delicately molded facial features; a fine red line that describes the curve of each eye socket; and the even blackness of the hair. Doll ht: 15in (38cm)

Layers of overglaze give a deep, smooth sheen

PRESSED PORCELAIN (LEFT) This
c.1840 German shoulder head is unusual in its flesh pink coloring. The hair, which shows rounded side panels covering the ears and a tightly knotted bun at the back of the head, is modeled after a style associated with the young English queen, Victoria. Head ht: 9in (23cm)

Entire head is covered with a tinted underglaze

Front shoulder plate is slightly shaped to form a rounded bosom

Untinted head, with brightly painted, "rouged" cheeks

Wavy hair falls in loose curls and ringlets

Uneven thickness of the material indicates a pressed head

Brush-marked hair detail at sides of face

Painted eyes, with black upper lids and brick red shadow-line above

Sloping shoulder plate is sewn to a stuffed cloth torso

ONE OF A PAIR (ABOVE)
Although styled in the same way, the black coloring of this c.1865 German lady's hair gives the doll a different appearance from that of its companion, shown in a back view below. Doll ht: 17½in (45cm)

REAR VIEW (ABOVE) As the 19th century
progressed, plain hairstyles soon gave way to more elaborate models. These ringlets and braided, coiled bun belong to the c.1850 German doll at right.
Ht: 4in (10cm)

Different shades of color suggest fine hair texture

Hair is held loosely tucked up at the back of the head

Tassels are adorned with a layer of lustrous gold paint

GILDED SNOOD (LEFT)
Popular in the 1860s and 1870s, snoods kept long hair neatly in place and decorated a lady's head at the same time. This one, seen on a c.1865 head, contains hair of a golden brown color, also known as café au lait. Doll ht: 12½in (32cm)

C.1850 DRAPED HAIRSTYLE WITH RINGLETS (ABOVE)
Changing tastes softened the 1840s sculptural "Queen Victoria" look into less severe styles. Few other changes were made to the doll, which still had the shoulder head attached by strong thread to a cloth body, often with kid arms. Ht: 16in (40cm)

Plain Glazed China Heads

· 1840s to 1870s ·

SOME PORCELAIN DOLL HEADS are marked, but the maker is not known; others are unmarked. Where a mark exists, it often appears on the inside of the shoulder plate. Many of these heads are still sewn to their original bodies and cannot be examined, as damaging the threads to remove the head from the body would divest the doll of much of its historical and collectible value. Occasionally, a porcelain head is found that has never been used with a body. As so few makers have been identified, the information that can be gleaned from such heads makes them as valuable as complete dolls. Not all doll heads were designed to show the ornate, elaborate hairstyles of fashionable ladies. Some have very simply modeled hair, with molded curls and painted feathering. These dolls with less decorative hairstyles generally portray boys, children, or babies.

Molded and painted hair, with side parting

Fine lines indicate upper eyelid and eye socket detail

Underglaze painted facial features

Closed mouth, colored orange, with darker shading between lips

Tape sewn around upper arms reinforces and hides the joins

Sleeves conceal glazed china arms, cast to above elbow

Oval blue ink stamp reads "Fr.H & Co./ Patent"

Binding around middle gives definition to the unshaped torso

Hands have molded, joined fingers and separate thumbs

Stitched seams at hips allow doll to sit securely on its rump

Clothing is from the doll's original wardrobe, part of which was bought at Izzard, a London toy store

Painted pink garter band, tied in a bow

Feet are shaped and painted to represent flat-heeled black ankle boots

Glazed china lower legs; left leg is a replacement of a slightly different size

Houndstooth check tweed trousers, with button-fly front

"ALLAN ALBERT" This c.1861 glazed china shoulder head is sewn to a Fischer, Naumann and Co. stuffed cloth body. The front of the torso bears the ink stamp of Franz Haas and Co. Haas was probably the London sales agent for Fischer, Naumann, a German company. In 1860, Haas applied for a British patent for a cloth body that enabled the doll to sit.

HT: 18in (46cm)

Very small head; hairstyle is that of a young man

Shoulder head is attached to a stuffed cloth torso and legs

High-quality pressed head is finely molded

The ink stamp, used c.1850, appears inside the shoulder plate. It shows a spread eagle encircled with the words "KOENIGL. PORZELLAN MANUFACTUR."

Molded hair, with feathered painting around the face

Flesh-colored tint covers the whole head

Sloping shoulders

HEAD OF A YOUTH

(ABOVE) *The Königliche Porzellan Manufaktur is one of the few known makers of porcelain heads. This example of its design for a youth's head, made in the 1850s, is unfinished because of a firing flaw. Head ht: 5in (13cm)*

BOY WITH LONG LEGS

(LEFT) *With its elongated limbs and shoulder head measuring a mere 3in (7.5cm) high, this 1860s German doll has an odd but endearing appearance. The kid arms have hands shaped as fists, with no fingers or thumbs. Ht: 16in (40cm)*

FLESH-TINTED HEAD (ABOVE)

Sometimes the same heads were used for dolls representing babies as well as older children. This c.1850 German head of an infant or child is marked with an "R" on the inside of the shoulder plate. Head ht: 3¼in (8cm)

Painted cobalt blue eyes, with black pupils

Pressed shoulder head

Informal smoking jacket, with wing-collared shirt and silk cravat

RARE HEAD (ABOVE)

It is the coloring that makes this head unusual: it has purple-rose shadings above the eyes, below the mouth and at its corners, and on the ears; and the hair and eyebrows are dark brown — more common from the 1860s, but still less usual than black. It was made in the 1860s to late 1870s, probably in France. Doll ht: 9in (23cm)

C.1865 GERMAN FLANGE NECK HEAD (RIGHT)

Relatively few flange neck heads were made: the majority of glazed china heads have shoulder plates. This example has molded blond curls rather than the usual head of dark hair. Its face is modeled to show the facial features of a baby. Ht: 6¼in (16cm)

Stuffed cloth upper limbs and torso

Doll wears its original clothes

Glazed china lower legs

Feet are molded to show joined toes

Painted pale blue eyes

Cleft, slightly double, chin

Glazed china lower arms; fingers are curved toward palms

Hands are fists, with stitched fingers; stiff leather body

MINIATURE DOLL (RIGHT)

This diminutive figure of a young man, made in Germany c.1850s–1860s, has a flesh-tinted glazed china shoulder head. It is possibly a dolls' house doll. Underglaze painting gives the doll delicately rosy cheeks, violet blue and black eyes, and wispy locks of brown hair. Ht: 5in (13cm)

Fancy Untinted Bisque Heads

· 1860s to 1880s ·

BY 1860, A MATTE PORCELAIN called untinted bisque began to replace glazed china. These later heads are sometimes also known as "parian," particularly in the United States, where the term has been used ever since the 1930s. "Parian" in fact refers to a variety of porcelain that was developed in the late 1840s by two English pottery factories, Minton and Copeland. This new porcelain, whose special properties gave it the luminous quality of white Parian marble, was probably never used for making doll heads, as it was very expensive to produce. The word "parian" did appear in many advertisements, perhaps as a sales ploy.

Untinted bisque heads lack the glossy finish of the glazed chinas, but are otherwise quite similar. They are usually white, except for the coloring of the facial features, and represent either ladies or men and children, according to the style of the molded hair.

Blue bead decoration is molded with the hair

Painted eyes, with black pupils and fine line below blue irises

Darker line between lips gives mouth slightly down-turned corners

Blond hair is molded into high braids around head

Molded bead decoration accentuates horseshoe shape above

Bead earrings, threaded on wire through pierced ears

Seersucker cotton blouse, with lace trim at neck and cuffs

Stuffed cloth upper arms

Two sew holes in back and front of shoulder plate

Hands have rounded, stuffed palms

Simply shaped hands; lines of stitching show fingers and thumbs

Cloth torso, shaped and stuffed to make a rounded sitting rump and narrow waist

Leather lower arms

Stuffed cloth upper legs

Stout lower legs, made to resemble blue stockings

Velvet-trimmed plum wool skirt

Heeled maroon leather boots, with buttoned fastening at sides

Box-pleated hem, decorated with silk velvet ribbons

C.1890 GERMAN LADY *The mark of Alt, Beck and Gottschalck — a company founded near Ohrdruf, Germany, in 1856 — is incised on the back of this fine untinted-bisque shoulder head. The cloth body with leather arms is similar to a type patented in 1878 by Mary Steuber of Philadelphia, Pennsylvania.*

HT: 20in (50cm)

Inset blue glass eyes, with black lashes and feathered blond brows

Pearl and gold bead earrings through pierced ears

Hair is molded to show looped curls

Copper luster finish on plume, giving it a metallic shine

1870s GERMAN GIRL (LEFT)

With its head marked "4 L 7," this doll is thought to be the work of C.F. Kling and Co. of Ohrdruf, Germany. The deep shoulder plate is sewn by three holes on either side to a stuffed cloth body.
Ht: 19in (48cm)

Leather lower arms; separate stitched fingers and thumbs

Hair is crimped into waves over forehead and curled and set in coils at back of head

Leather boots sewn to checked stockings form the lower legs

Unmarked German head, made late 1870s to early 1880s

UNTINTED BISQUE HEAD WITH MOLDED HAT (LEFT)

The chic molded hairstyles of lady doll heads were often adorned with trimmings, such as bows, or more elaborate confections. This 1860s German doll wears an elegant hat tipped low over a head of luxuriant blond hair. Doll ht: 10in (25cm)

Shoulder head is sewn to a stuffed cloth body, with bisque lower limbs; lower legs are molded to show flat-heeled boots

GERMAN HEAD WITH TIARA (LEFT)

Lusterware — porcelain with luster decoration — was greatly admired during the second half of the 19th century. Its popularity is reflected in the headdress of this delicately featured untinted bisque shoulder head, made c.1860.
Head ht: 5½in (14cm)

Gold earrings are painted onto ears

Feathered eyebrows and painted lashes

Molded black bow

Blond molded hair

Dress conceals stuffed cloth upper limbs and torso

Regional costume is hand-sewn

STYLISH REAR VIEW (RIGHT)

The back of a hairstyle can almost be more decorative than the front, as this immaculately presented 1870s coiffure shows. The German doll to which it belongs has an untinted bisque shoulder head on a cloth body.
Doll ht: 12in (30cm)

Pierced ears, with rosy lobes and gold earrings

Shoulders are tinted flesh pink

PATTERNED SHOULDER HEAD (LEFT)

This impressive example of porcelain molding and painting has thick braids of blond hair set high on the crown of the head, and two tiny kiss-curls to soften the forehead. Around the doll's throat is a black "velvet" neckband with a drop pendant. The tucked bodice sports ribbons, bows, and lace. Ht: 24in (60cm)

SIMON AND HALBIG LADY (RIGHT)

The mark "S 0 H" on the front of the shoulder plate identifies this head as one made by this famous firm. Inset glass eyes and bisque lower limbs, with the lower legs molded to show heeled boots and blue garter ribbons, all date the doll c.1870s. Ht: 12in (30cm)

Plain Untinted Bisque Heads

· 1860s to 1880s ·

UNTINTED BISQUE DOLL HEADS made around the end of the 1860s were often designed to show neat, flat hairstyles that were usually molded quite close to the crown, with a central part. Popularly known as flat-topped heads, most portray children or older boys. Heads that represent ladies were still produced, but in smaller quantities. Like the heads of the children and boys, the lady heads also show hairstyles that are far simpler than the crimped waves, exuberant curls, and coiled braids of the earlier models.

A noteworthy feature of the later dolls is the increasing use of bisque for the lower limbs, which are modeled in a fairly convincing manner. Particular attention was given to the legs, with the tiny feet molded and then painted to show fashionable boots.

Center parting is faintly indicated; no indent or white line

Painted blue eyes, with black pupils; light brown painted brows

Painted red mouth, with darker crossline and full lower lip

Inner eye corners and nostrils are highlighted with dots of red paint

Head is modeled to show a short, childlike neck and dimples beneath the collarbone

Two sew holes in front and back of shoulder plate

Doll wears a striped jacket over a coarse cotton undershirt

Hands have separate thumbs and inward-curving fingers

Cloth upper arms

Bisque lower arms; thumbs show vertical casting lines

Stitching at joins between upper cloth and lower bisque legs allows the limbs to bend

Cloth upper legs and torso, shaped at waist; internal wire frame and sawdust stuffing

Breeches match the jacket

Bisque lower legs are short and chunky, but well shaped

Painted boots on male dolls can have "elastic" at sides or "laced" fronts

Small heels – a post-1860 fashion style – help to date the doll

Decorative lower legs

UNTINTED BISQUE HEAD WITH BISQUE LOWER LIMBS *The flowing blond curls of this c.1865 German shoulder head are typical of styles worn by young boys in the second half of the 19th century, when male children had long hair well beyond babyhood. The lower legs end in minute feet, shaped and decorated as fashionable heeled boots.*

Painted pink garter ribbons

Purple-colored copper luster finish on ankle boots

HT: 10in (25cm)

Eyes lack socket lines and dots at corners

Poor-quality untinted bisque shoulder head

1860S BOY WITH FLAT BOOTS (LEFT) Poorer quality porcelain heads have a slightly grainy appearance and are sometimes described as "stoneware." The example shown here was made in Germany. Boots without heels were a popular style of footwear for both sexes before 1860. Ht: 9in (23cm)

Stuffed cloth upper limbs and torso

INTAGLIO EYES (RIGHT) The usual practice of molding painted eyes as convex shapes is reversed for intaglio eyes, which are concave – a style that was inherited from statuary carvings. Although intaglio eyes are a common feature of the later Gebrüder Heubach character heads, no other features of this German c.1870 untinted bisque shoulder head suggest that this famous firm was the maker. Doll ht: 15in (38cm)

Deep curls and ringlets

Eye sockets are heavily shadowed

Shoulder plate is molded as a blouse

Curls extend around back of head

1860S GERMAN HEAD (LEFT) A slight irregularity in the facial features adds a charming naïveté to this untinted bisque shoulder head. Its mouth is finely modeled, with the somewhat downturned corners of a child's face in repose. Doll ht: 17in (43cm)

SCOTS BOY (BELOW) With its molded hair painted brown, this costume doll possibly dates between 1870 and 1875: hair colored either brown or blond may indicate a later head. The eyes are molded to show heavy lids over large black pupils and pale blue irises. Ht: 8½in (22cm)

Bisque lower arms, hands are simply modeled

Shoulders slope sharply away from the neck

C.1875 SWIVEL HEAD (RIGHT) Representing a young girl, this swivel head was probably made by the famous German doll manufacturer Simon and Halbig. It has especially striking, luminous dark blue painted eyes, framed by black lashes and feathered eyebrows. The full, orange-red lips, separated by a crimson crossline, almost appear to smile. Doll ht: 9in (23cm)

Feathered, light brown eyebrows

Pale red mouth, with darker highlights

Painted flat-heeled boots

Ceramic lower legs, cast to above knees

Feathered eyebrows follow the shape of the eye sockets

Painted black upper and lower eyelashes

Inset blue glass eyes

Rosebud mouth

Neck fits into the separately cast shoulder plate, allowing head to turn

Hands have stitched fingers and separate thumbs

LADY WITH GLASS EYES (RIGHT) The hair of this c.1870s shoulder head is styled into rows of ringlets and deep fronds over the forehead that provide a nice balance to the head's square jaw. Delicately painted facial features complement the doll's deep blue glass eyes. Doll ht: 12in (30cm)

Molded and painted tassel

Heel and boot upper are painted to look like leather

BISQUE DETAIL (LEFT) The Lady with Glass Eyes at left has a stuffed cloth torso and upper limbs, and lower limbs of bisque. The lower legs are molded and painted to show gaiter-type boots, with a scalloped side-button fastening. Worn by young women of the smart set, they have toes designed to fit only the daintiest of fashionably small feet.

Sporran is made of horse or deer hair

Bisque Dolls

Doll language gives the name "bisque" to a type of porcelain that has been fired twice, with color added — both as an overall tint and as detailed highlights — before the second firing. The difference between bisque heads and other porcelain types lies in the finish: though glazed, bisque does not have the glossy sheen of the glazed chinas; neither has it the matte texture and marblelike whiteness of most untinted bisque heads.

BISQUE BECAME AN INCREASINGLY POPULAR material for doll heads in the mid-nineteenth century, and it remained so until the 1930s. Bisque heads were expensive to make, but if produced in large quantities, could be cost-effective. Many of the German factories that produced bisque heads, limbs, and complete dolls were already manufacturing porcelain or earthenware household items. Some were almost cottage industries, with only a single kiln. Others were much larger, having workshops covering several acres. Most were in Thuringia, a region in eastern Germany that had abundant supplies of raw clay and wood. Cheap labor was available, too.

~ To make a bisque head, a clay mixture was cast in a two- or three-part, usually plaster,

mold. The molds were carefully scrutinized prior to the casting, as any flaws would be reproduced in the castings. Each mold was used only 40 or 50 times before it was discarded. Early heads were made of a stiff clay "paste" pressed into the molds; later, a pourable, semi-liquid clay slip was perfected. This slip produced heads with a smoother surface and allowed greater refinement in the modeling of facial features than was possible using the pressed material.

~ When firmly set, the doll head or other part (called greenware in its prefired state) was removed from the mold. The casting lines were cleaned, it was fired, colored, and fired again. The heads needed special supports while in the kilns, because they

C.1880 BÉBÉ JUMEAU (LEFT) *Finding a famous-name, marked doll, with its original clothing and packaging, is a real joy. This bébé has a pressed bisque head and a composition and wood body, stamped "BÉBÉ JUMEAU Bte. S.G.D.G. DÉPOSÉ." Ht: 31in (80cm)*

POST-1910 INDIAN GIRL (RIGHT) *This charming figure is one of Simon and Halbig's "Dolls of Four Races." Its bisque socket head, composition body, flirty glass eyes, and human hair wig are all colored to represent a girl from India. Ht: 12in (30cm)*

WALTERSHAUSEN WORKSHOP

(LEFT) Kämmer and Reinhardt was founded in 1886 by doll designer Ernst Kämmer and salesman Franz Reinhardt. The left-hand side of the photograph at left shows the painting of doll heads at one of its workshops in Waltershausen, Germany, using a new technique developed by the company. The right-hand side of the photograph shows the making of human hair eyelashes. This was also a Kämmer and Reinhardt innovation.

ASSEMBLING THE DOLLS

(LEFT) Another photograph taken in one of Kämmer and Reinhardt's Waltershausen workshops shows a selection of bisque heads and composition bodies, ready to be put together. The finishing of the dolls was always done in the factory, but outworkers were hired for other parts of the production process, such as making the blown glass eyes. Kämmer and Reinhardt produced numerous doll designs, including a successful line of character dolls.

C.1897 GIRL (ABOVE) This J.D. Kestner doll has what is known as a "bald head." Beneath the wig, the pate has not been cut away for the insertion of the eyes. Ht: 18in (46cm)

were liable to sag on their necks when water in the porcelain slip evaporated during the initial firing.

The first heads made had molded hair and eyes, and closed mouths. Later heads have glass eyes, either inset, or the lead-weighted sleeping or flirty type. For these, the eye sockets were cut out and shaped at the greenware stage. Molded ears, teeth, and tongues were usually designed as part of the mold, but inset teeth (produced in quantity by the Simon and Halbig company) were made separately and glued into the mouth before the final dressing of the head.

Investigating the Facts

Today, there is some confusion about where and when bisque doll heads were made, and by whom. Many of the incised marks on bisque heads are unclear, and some trademarks, too, are often very similar to one another, making it hard to identify the true maker. What *is* known is that far more bisque doll heads were produced in Thuringia than anywhere else. The production of some French factories, such as Jumeau and Steiner, is also well documented, and it is probable that German firms occasionally met the production needs of French factories whose output was oversubscribed. Large numbers of bisque heads were

exported and attached to their "foreign" bodies later: a German head on a French body, dressed in England, for example, is still considered to be an original doll. Nowadays, a doll's country of origin is given as the country in which its head was made, as it is in the head that the doll's "personality" is conveyed.

There is little doubt that France and Germany dominated the international market for bisque doll heads, limbs, and complete dolls until 1914, when World War I interrupted their manufacturing. England produced rather poor quality stoneware, as opposed to porcelain, doll parts; and dolls from Japan, though made of porcelain, fell far below the very high standards set by France and Germany.

1920S ENGLISH STONEWARE HEAD

(RIGHT) Glass eyes were usually inserted into ceramic heads by cutting away the crown, setting the eyes, and then replacing the cut section with a piece of cork – a very neat operation that was completely concealed beneath the doll's wig. Head ht: 4in (10cm)

Fashionable Lady Dolls

· 1860s to 1890s ·

FASHION DOLLS – stylish representations of elegant young ladies in *haute couture* – were at their most popular between 1860 and 1890. Although most came from France, many were merely assembled there, using swivel heads or shoulder heads imported from German porcelain makers on French-made bodies. While many heads are unmarked, and others bear figures or characters that are not identified as the marks of any known maker, it is thought that some well-known French factories, such as Jumeau and Bru, did produce bisque heads.

Dolls of this type usually have inset (rarely sleeping) oval or almond-shaped glass eyes. Their stuffed kid bodies are skilfully pieced together in sections to recreate the undulating curves of a young woman wearing a tightly laced, boned corset.

Ash blonde mohair wig (a modern replacement) is pinned to the original cork pate

Painted eyebrows and lashes

Inset glass eyes are pale blue, with a darker outer rim

Pierced ears

Closed mouth

Sleeves conceal shoulder plate, marked "4" on the edge

Original strawberry blonde mohair wig

Pale bisque swivel head, with typically long face and full cheeks

Inset brown glass eyes are a striking feature; blue eyes are usual

Elbows have V-shaped gussets so that arms can bend

Stuffed kid arms, torso, and legs, in excellent condition

Top of kid torso is glued over the bisque shoulder plate

Arms, legs, and torso are made of firmly stuffed kid

Hands have separate fingers and thumbs

Thumbs and fingers are separate

On back of doll: large gussets between rump and upper thighs allow limited movement

Stockings, pinned to legs, cover gussets at backs of knees

Sawdust-stuffed body; internal wire frame gives support

Sewn-on shoes hide simply shaped feet

Striped silk dress, with heavy velvet collar and sleeve trim

C.1875 FRENCH LADIES At 33cm (13in) high, the undressed doll shown here is somewhat shorter than its dressed companion, though the two are otherwise quite similar. Their bisque swivel heads have socket necks set into the bisque shoulder plates, which allow the heads to be attractively angled.

HT: 46cm (18in)

SUMMER OUTFIT (*LEFT*) The rounded face and sweetly innocent facial expression of this c.1875 French Belton-type shoulder head indicate that the doll was intended to represent a young girl rather than a lady. It sports the pierced ears – here threaded with blue bead earrings – seen on most of the fashion dolls. Ht: 15in (38cm)

Inset large blue-gray glass eyes

Closed mouth

Gusseted kid arms, torso, and legs

Simple cotton outfit, topped with a flower-trimmed straw hat, suits the doll's childlike appearance

UNDERGARMENTS A LA MODE (*RIGHT*) Attributed to Margueritte Frène of Caen, France, this bisque shoulder head dates from the late 1870s. The doll has two rare features: the vibrant coloring of the cheeks; and the closed, upturned "smiling" mouth. Ht: 26in (65cm)

Chestnut brown human hair wig

Painted chin highlights echo those of the cheeks

Stuffed kid arms, with gussets at elbows

Separate fingers and thumbs

Period undergarments cover the stuffed kid body and legs; gussets at hips and knees

Flat-soled feet have separate toes

FOOTWEAR FOR LADIES (*BELOW*) The fine accessories of fashion dolls were handcrafted with as much attention to detail as the real-life items they copied. These tiny leather shoes are for cloth or kid feet. Dolls with bisque lower legs have molded and painted feet to suggest boots.

Ostrich feathers, dyed blue to match stripes in dress

c.1875 leather shoe, with high back and buttoned ankle strap

Molded bisque gaiter-type boot, with tassel top: foot detail of lady at right

Post-1875 pink-tinted bisque shoulder head

Inset blue glass eyes; fine lines radiate from pupils to edges of irises

TEA ON THE LAWN (*RIGHT*) Dolls with heads that turn and movable limbs have great appeal. This 1870s French lady has a bisque swivel head. The hips and knees have V-shaped gussets that allow the limbs to be placed in a variety of positions. Ht: 12½in (32cm)

Silk and lace parasol, with brass fittings

Inset blue glass eyes have very large pupils

Promenade dress, made of net woven with stripes of blue satin

Bisque lower arms; hands have joined fingers and separate thumbs

Pale pink bisque lower arms

Dress conceals sawdust-filled cotton body

GIRL WITH PAINTED BOOTS (*RIGHT*) Made in France after 1875, this doll is thought to have been created by doll-maker Huret. The short dress indicates that the doll represents a girl rather than a lady. A detail of the doll's bisque lower leg is shown in close-up above. Ht: 19in (48cm)

Close-up of boot is shown above

Developments in Body Types

· 1860s to 1880s ·

THE 20 YEARS BETWEEN 1860 and 1880 were halcyon days for the fashionably dressed dolls of France and Germany, and manufacturers ensured their continuing popularity by making increasingly realistic bodies for the dolls' fine bisque heads. Bisque lower arms and sometimes legs replaced stuffed kid limbs, and though early models are clumsy compared to the delicately stitched kid, later castings are more refined. The articulation of doll bodies was a new challenge, and it was here that the greatest advances were made.
~ The French firm Gesland operated in Paris from 1860 to 1928. The jointed metal frame of its padded stockinette body allowed the limbs and torso to assume and retain a variety of positions, and was a major innovation of this particular period.

Light blond mohair wig

Pierced ears

Beneath padding, left side of shoulder plate bears Gaultier's mark, "F.G."

Doll wears a contemporary walking outfit of white silk; collar trimmed with broderie anglaise forms a shoulder cape

Swivel head can be turned on its shoulder plate

Padded arms conceal wire frame, which allows elbows to bend

Back of torso is stamped with Gesland's mark

Bisque hands, cast to just above wrist joints

Upper legs, torso, and arms made of stockinette, padded with wool fiber, over a wire frame

Deep border of broderie anglaise on French cuffs

Shapely lower legs, made of bisque

Flat feet, with molded toes

Petticoat and undergarments are made of matching broderie anglaise

Eight mother-of-pearl buttons fasten the coat

High-heeled, laced black leather boots, with brown leather facings and soles

GESLAND BODY WITH GAULTIER HEAD

Cooperative agreements were a common practice within the doll industry, especially where parts made of different materials were teamed together. This c.1880 lady has a bisque swivel head, hands, and lower legs made by Gaultier of Paris and a Gesland padded stockinette body over a wire armature.

HT: 24in (60cm)

White
mohair wig

Long, waisted
jacket of
purple silk,
with square
scallop detail
at hem

Kid hands have
well-shaped,
separate fingers
and thumbs

Original
striped silk
skirt, showing
damage by
sunlight

C.1866 "MANUELITA"
(ABOVE) This elegant French lady
doll has a body of stuffed kid and a
pale bisque swivel head, with inset
almond-shaped dark blue glass eyes,
and a mohair wig. Ht: 15in (38cm)

BISQUE-HEADED TWINS (RIGHT)
Probably of German origin, this pair was
made toward the end of the 1870s. The
naked figure is a fine example of a kid doll
body of the late 1800s. Other materials
were also available, but high-quality bodies
were usually made of kid.
Ht: 18in (46cm)

Inset blue glass
eyes, with painted
lashes and brows

Torso, upper arms,
and legs are made
of wood covered
with kid

Bisque
lower
arms

Tenon
joints at
elbows
and waist

Joints at
hips, so doll
can sit easily

Joints at ankles and knees
for optimum movement

Bisque swivel
head

Promenade
costume,
made of silk

Thick mohair
wig dressed in
braids, pinned
to a cork pate

Close-fitting,
short-waisted
jacket, with
flared sleeves

Bustle and
train at
back of
skirt

Flat-fronted
skirt: a late
1870s style

Brown mohair wig
over a cork pate

Shoulder plate is
molded to show a
high bosom

V-shaped
gussets at
elbows

Finely made
kid hands, with
long fingers

Elaborate, two-
tiered train, edged
with checked
quilting
and lace

Lower eye
sockets have dark
painted rims

THE BRIDE (LEFT) Fashion dolls
are unrivaled in displaying the styles
of the period. Here, a doll with a
French or German bisque shoulder
head and kid body models an 1880s
bridal gown. Ht: 14in (35cm)

C.1870 BARROIS LADY (RIGHT) The
mark "E. Déposé B.," which is incised on
this doll's front shoulder plate, is that of
E. Barrois. Porcelain factories in both
France and Germany produced heads
for this famous Parisian company
between 1844 and 1877.
Ht: 12½in (32cm)

Lace-trimmed, cream
satin gown, with pleats,
bows, and flounces

Arched feet
have toes
indicated
with lines
of stitching

Bisque
shoulder head

Closed mouth

Blond fleece
wig, with
skin backing

Inset azure blue
glass eyes

Dress conceals
stuffed kid
upper arms,
torso, and legs

Bisque lower
arms, with
molded fingers
and thumbs

Satin-trimmed
muslin skirt over
a hooped crinoline

Jumeau Dolls

· 1842 to 1958 ·

PIERRE FRANÇOIS JUMEAU established his company in Paris in 1842, originally making wood or kid doll bodies and doll clothes. In 1867, his son, Emile, joined the firm, bringing a fresh spirit of commercial enterprise. The company expanded, and in 1873 began to make bisque doll heads, cast at its factory outside Paris in Montreuil-sous-Bois. Soon after, Emile introduced the *bébés Jumeau* – dolls with fine bisque heads, jointed composition bodies, and an innocent expression. Their quality and appeal did much to establish Jumeau's reputation.

Faced with increasing competition from German doll-makers, Jumeau amalgamated with other French companies in 1899 to form the *Société Française de Fabrication de Bébés et Jouets* (S.F.B.J.). Both name and company survived within the *Société* until trading came to an end in 1958.

Matching velvet bonnet, trimmed with dyed ostrich feathers

Inset pale blue glass eyes; fine lines radiating from pupils give lifelike effect

Lower eyelashes are detailed with precise brushstrokes

Dark blond mohair wig, curled into corkscrews over forehead

Bisque socket head

Rosebud mouth, deeply indented, darker highlights accentuate the fine molding of the lips

Long silk tunic dress, with silk checked collar

Wood and composition arms, ball-jointed at elbows and shoulders

Marked composition torso, molded to show a rounded belly and chest

Childlike, chubby hands, with short fingers and thumbs

Doll wears its original outfit, a tunic dress; front facings form two false pockets at hem

Composition legs, with ball joints at knees and hips

Whole body is varnished over five layers of flesh-tone paint

Pleated silk "skirt," trimmed with lace

Long toes are molded together, but still well defined

Petticoat is edged with handmade lace

Machine-knitted socks, made of mercerized cotton

BÉBÉ JUMEAU *The inspiration for the bébés Jumeau is said to have come from a portrait of Henri IV of France, aged four. Whatever the source, their insouciant charm has won the hearts of buyers and collectors since the first doll was sold. This example dates from between 1880 and 1885, and shows the exceptionally fine quality of Jumeau dolls manufactured before 1899.*

Faded maroon leather shoes are stamped on soles "EJUMEAU/ MED OR/ 1876/ PARIS/DÉPOSÉ"

Silk rosettes match the rest of the doll's outfit

HT: 22in (55cm)

"FLORENCE" (RIGHT)
Named by her original
child owner, "Florence" is a
large bébé of late 1880s
or early 1890s vintage.
Like all the bébés, the
doll has a bisque socket
head and a papier-mâché
composition body, jointed
at the shoulders, elbows,
hips, and knees so that
the limbs can be moved
into various positions.
The head and body
are both marked (see
Doll Marks, right).
Ht: 30in (75cm)

*Strawberry blond
mohair wig*

*Large inset blue
glass eyes*

*White line suggests
a row of teeth*

Pierced ears

*Salmon pink velvet dress
is a later purchase; dolls
were often sold unclothed*

*Cork pate fits
snugly into
head cavity*

*Glass eyes
inserted
through
cut section*

*Socket head
turns easily
to either side*

HEAD PROFILE (ABOVE)
Carefully removing the mohair wig
from the head of "Florence" reveals
the cork pate to which it was pinned
– a method of attaching hair that
was used for most Jumeau dolls. The
profile also shows two other features:
the realistic modeling of the molded
ears, and the bulbous, luminous
blown glass eyes (sometimes called
paperweight eyes).

DOLL MARKS
These ink stamps are from
the doll "Florence"; they are
usually found together.

Patented head details include
the size: "14" indicates a
height of 30in (75cm).

DÉPOSÉ
TÊTE JUMEAU
Bᵗᵉ S.G.D.G.
14

Body mark refers to the 1885
Paris Exhibition – the doll
was awarded the gold medal.

JUMEAU
MÉDAILLE D'OR
PARIS

C.1875 FASHION DOLL (LEFT)
Though unmarked, this doll is of a
type also associated with Jumeau. Its
bisque swivel head, with inset glass
eyes, pierced ears, and blond
mohair wig, and its gusseted,
stuffed kid, internally wired
body are common features
of fashion dolls made from
1860 to 1880. The doll
wears a silk walking
outfit and side-
buttoning leather
boots in period style.
Ht: 14in (35cm)

*The bee trade-
mark, stamped on
the soles of some
doll shoes made
by Jumeau, was
registered in 1891.*

*Stockings conceal
bisque lower legs*

*Blond mohair
wig, styled
in ringlets*

*Inset pale blue
glass eyes*

*Fingers of
right hand are
curved to hold
a parasol*

FRENCH NURSEMAID (LEFT)
This mechanical doll has an
unmarked bisque swivel head,
probably made by Jumeau between
1880 and 1890. Inside its body is
a Roullet and Decamps wind-up
mechanism, which is wound with a
key projecting from the doll's right
hip. The nursemaid and mailcart –
the vehicle holding the baby – are
joined together, allowing the entire
ensemble to move forward as the
doll "walks." Ht: 12in (30cm)

*Fringed silk canopy,
now very worn*

*Baby is all-bisque, jointed
at shoulders and hips*

*Bent arms, with
hands shaped as fists*

*Metal mailcart – a
type of stroller*

*Bisque lower
legs, molded
and painted
to show
heeled boots*

Lady with Wooden Body

· 1870s ·

A VARIETY OF DIFFERENT STYLES OF DOLL were made during the 1870s, as companies vied with each other to produce the very best models showing the most innovative designs. Dolls that could walk, talk, throw kisses, or even do all three at once, found eager buyers; but against all the competition, a model of enduring popularity emerged: the doll with a fine bisque swivel head and matching shoulder plate attached to a shapely body. Many attempts were made to create the ideal body – an objective that proved elusive until the development of fully jointed types. In 1872, Bru Jne. and Cie. issued a product catalog listing doll bodies made of stuffed kid or a combination of kid and wood. It also included a marvelous new design – an all-wooden lady doll body (quite similar to the one shown here) resembling an artist's mannequin, and using two different varieties of joint to provide maximum movement for the limbs.

Reddish blond human hair wig

Closed mouth; darker paint detail highlights bow of the lips

Bisque swivel head, lightly tinted to resemble fine white skin

Neck socket is lined with kid, to prevent chafing as head turns

Inset blue glass eyes

Cotton chemise top; front fastens with cotton-covered buttons

Flange joints allow lower arms to rotate

Band of kid covers the join between bisque shoulder plate and wooden torso

Mortise and tenon joints at shoulders

Mortise and tenon joints at elbows

Wooden parts are painted flesh pink and varnished

Wooden torso, carved to show narrow waist, buxom hips, and flattened bosom

Mortise and tenon joints at hips

Ball and socket joints at wrists

Boned cotton twill corset, shaped to the doll's torso

Flaking paint exposes bare wood beneath

Longish, nicely rounded thighs

Flange joints at mid-upper legs, so lower legs can rotate

Mortise and tenon joints at knees

Split drawers with open crotch, made in one piece with the chemise

Bottoms of feet are arched between ankles and toes

HT: 22in (55cm)

C.1870 ARTICULATED LADY *This elegant, carved wooden body, designed specifically for lady dolls, re-creates the "ideal" look of the 1870s, when a rounded body with small waist was considered the most attractive female shape. Compared to the curvaceous torso, the doll's limbs appear rather unrefined, though the feet are surprisingly detailed.*

Deep notches separate the toes

Delicately modeled feet

Rounded lid provides extra space for topmost items packed inside

Parchment paper and "ivory" fan, painted with white edelweiss

Lace-trimmed satin peignoir – a type of dressing gown

TRAVELING BOX (LEFT)

The lady's wardrobe of fashionable outfits, undergarments, and accessories is conveniently housed inside a Saratoga trunk – a round-lidded case frequently used by ladies when traveling. This miniature replica of a full-sized trunk is made of wood covered in leather cloth, with leather bindings and metal fittings. A removable tray (see below) fits snugly within the body of the trunk. The lining paper is printed with brightly colored candy stripes – a favorite late 19th-century design.

Feather-stitching attaches the lace trim

Pretty short-sleeved summer dress, made of printed muslin

Strap secured to lid and base

Metal carrying handles at sides

Back view of doll's corset, with laced eyelet fastening

LIFT-OUT TRAY (BELOW)

The more fragile items and those that might damage the clothing are kept in the trunk's removable tray. Stored in the front section are (left to right) two pairs of leather walking boots; stoppered glass bottles for perfume and toilet waters; a leather purse; diamanté jewelry on a satin reticule; and a mirror with filigree back.

Wicker jewelry box; base is lined with cotton

Embossed "silver" pendant necklet

"Pearl" and "jet" necklaces

Pink and black bead necklace, with bead drops

Straw hat, with braided brim and chiffon trim

Black lace and ribbon trim

Bonnet with ostrich feathers and ruched silk

LADY AT LEISURE (BELOW)

Writing letters was a popular pastime of wealthy young ladies in the 19th century. They would correspond about society, clothes, music, dancing, their travels, families, and their latest beaux.

Bone-handled umbrella, with cotton cover and metal fittings

Elbow-length kid gloves

Handmade writing paper

Matching envelopes, tied with original silk ribbon

Mirror-backed wooden hairbrush

Kid gloves

Tortoise-shell lorgnette

French miniature pocket watch

Wooden hairbrush, with real bristles

Tortoise-shell comb

Cotton parasol, with wooden handle

Steiner Dolls

· 1855 to 1908 ·

JULES NICHOLAS STEINER is probably better remembered for his company's wonderful mechanical dolls than for their intricate wind-up movements, which he also designed. A former clockmaker, Steiner founded the Steiner Société (also known as Steiner Cie.) in 1855. The company survived his death in 1891 and continued to trade until 1908, yet it was undoubtedly Steiner who provided the creative impetus for this Parisian business; during his leadership, the firm won several prizes. Along with the complex, expensive mechanical dolls, the Steiner Société produced simpler models and nonmechanical play dolls. All have bisque heads, which are thought to have been made in French porcelain factories, although the heads of the mechanical dolls rarely bear any company's mark.

Lace-trimmed silk bonnet, tied with silk velvet ribbons

Inset deep blue glass eyes

Open mouth, showing four teeth at top and bottom

Rosy pink tint on fingernails

White silk floss wig, pinned to a cork pate

Unmarked pale bisque shoulder head

Heavy metal armature at shoulders, for moving the arms

Upper arms of kid stretched over pressed cardboard

Kid-covered wooden torso ends at waist

Bisque lower arms, robustly modeled

Bisque lower arms are cast to well above elbows

Pasteboard bell forms the lower half of the doll

Metal frame within bell houses and protects the wind-up mechanism

Brass winding key

Printed cotton dress is designed to conceal the doll's working parts

Wooden base

Rivets attach the pasteboard bell to the base

1870S AUTOMATED LADY *The mechanism inside this doll is wound with a brass key and is activated by an on–off switch next to the key. The wheel can be set so the doll rotates or moves forward, simultaneously raising and lowering its arms and calling, "Mama!"*

HT: 15in (38cm)

Rotating wheel

Label of London doll-maker and seller Charles Marsh (see page 35)

On–off switch

Winding key

BASE DETAIL (LEFT) The three small wheels that protrude through the holes cut in the Automated Lady's wooden base have three separate functions: one stabilizes the doll; one is the drive wheel; and one sets its direction.

Stabilizer wheel

Drive wheel

Mohair wig, styled with side parting

Inset large blue glass eyes

Heavy, feathered eyebrows

Closed mouth

Bisque socket head, incised at back below hairline "J. STEINER/ BTE S.G.D.G./PARIS/ FiRE A 9"

Composition arms, jointed at shoulders and elbows

Label reads "LE PETIT PARISIEN/ BÉBÉ J.STEINER/ MARQUE DÉPOSÉE/ MÉDAILLE D'OR/ PARIS/1889"

Typical feature: fingers are all roughly the same length

Composition upper legs and torso, jointed at hips

Composition lower legs, jointed at knees

Space between big and smaller toes

STEINER KICKING DOLL
(BELOW) An unusual feature of the dressed doll pictured at bottom is revealed in this detail: a bisque head with flange neck, which fits over the metal bar that turns the head from side to side. The doll's inset deep blue glass eyes and open, toothed mouth are typical of Steiner automata.

Unjointed composition arms

Kid and composition torso

Torso houses the doll's mechanism

Head turns from side to side as doll moves

Beneath dress, key and lever activate the wind-up mechanism

DOLL MARKS
Mechanical dolls may be marked only on the wind-up mechanism itself.

The paper label on post-1889 dolls details the name, patent registration, and award date.

ARRESTED MOVEMENT (LEFT and BELOW) The Kicker – seen here in "action" – found a popular market in the United States and Europe between 1870 and 1890. The wind-up mechanism that controls its head, arms, and legs also enables the doll to utter a plaintive cry. Ht: 18in (46cm)

Blond mohair wig, with flat top and curls

POST-1890 BÉBÉ STEINER
(ABOVE) Steiner bébés are usually characterized by their pretty faces, with closed mouths and heavily painted eyebrows. Their bisque socket heads usually bear one of the Steiner marks incised on the nape of the neck. Ht: 15in (38cm)

Composition lower legs

Splay-toed feet are designed for kicking, rather than walking

The S.F.B.J. and Others

· 1899 to 1950s ·

DURING THE FINAL DECADES of the nineteenth century, more and more German dolls were imported into France, presenting a lively threat to the already competitive home market. Ten companies responded to this disquieting development by forming, in 1899, the *Société Française de Fabrication de Bébés et Jouets* (S.F.B.J.) – a union composed largely of French doll producers, including both Jumeau and Bru. Some German companies were also admitted, notably the country's largest single investor, Fleischmann and Bloedel.

~ In 1905, the S.F.B.J. registered its trademark: a circle divided into quarters, each segment containing one of the *Société's* four initials. Other marks on S.F.B.J. dolls use the same initials, with mold and size numbers.

S.F.B.J. dolls made after 1905 often have this printed paper label stuck to their bodies. The details on the label are usually repeated in the incised head marks.

Shoulder-length mohair wig, styled with a left-side parting

Pierced ears

Bisque socket head

Ball joints at wrists allow hands to rotate

Composition hands; separately molded fingers and thumbs

Composition legs

Roughly modeled feet: toes are barely distinguished

Silk hat with upturned brim; doll outfits usually included matching headwear

Top eyelashes are made of animal hair

Open mouth, with a row of molded top teeth, is characteristic of S.F.B.J. dolls

Composition arms, jointed at elbows

At back of torso, paper label is stuck to the left side

Composition body, jointed at hips and shoulders

Ball joints at knees give lower legs backward and sideways movement

Sleeping brown glass eyes; single-color eyes are an S.F.B.J. feature

Bottom eyelashes are painted

Dress is made from a lightweight fabric known as "washing silk"

Book bound in tooled leather is a tiny replica of a 1903 German diary

Wickerwork valise, with bound cane handles

Machine-crocheted cotton socks

Simple mercerized cotton ties

Cloth shoes, with cardboard-reinforced soles

C.1905 S.F.B.J. GIRL *Although many of the firms that joined the Société were renowned for the excellence of their products, dolls manufactured under the S.F.B.J. blanket were usually of a poorer quality. This early model, a typical example of dolls made soon after the trademark registration, reveals no clue as to which member of the Société produced it.*

HT: 14in (35cm)

Bisque socket head, marked
on back and neck

Inset blue-gray
glass eyes, with
dark pupils

Brown
mohair wig

C.1910 S.F.B.J. DOLLY FACE
GIRL (RIGHT) The bisque socket
head of this doll is incised on the back
below the hairline "S.F.B.J./PARIS/60"
and on the neck "2." The double figures
indicate that the head was made from
mold number 60 – a dolly face style
that was a best-seller for the Société.
The size, 2, corresponds to the height
of the doll. Ht: 20in (50cm)

Black
velvet dress

Composition arms, jointed at
wrists, shoulders, and elbows

A. LANTERNIER GIRL (BELOW)
Founded in 1855, the A. Lanternier
and Cie. porcelain factory in Limoges,
France, made bisque dolls and heads
from 1915 to 1924. The incised mark
on this head bears the doll's name,
Chérie. Other names on Lanternier
heads are Favorite, La Georgienne,
Toto, and Caprice. Ht: 27in (68cm)

Replacement
human hair wig

Inset
blue
glass
eyes

Bisque socket
head, marked
on back

Dress conceals
composition
body, jointed
at shoulders,
elbows, wrists,
hips, and knees

J. VERLINGUE BISQUE
SWIVEL HEAD (RIGHT) Some
companies did manage to survive
outside the S.F.B.J. The small
Parisian business of J. Verlingue
traded between 1915 and the
1920s. This head of one of its lady
dolls is teamed with a gusseted kid
body. Ht: 15in (38cm)

Pierced ears

Highly tinted bisque swivel
head and shoulder plate

Incised on the back of the head,
below the hairline, the mark reads
"PETITE FRANÇAISE/J V/FRANCE/1/
LIANE." The company's anchor
trademark can be seen between
the J and V.

Chestnut brown
mohair wig

Dress conceals
composition
legs,
jointed at hips
and knees

Swiss
cotton pinafore

Sleeping brown glass
eyes; top lashes are
made of animal hair

Open mouth, with
well-defined, molded
top teeth

Composition arms,
jointed at shoulders,
elbows, and wrists

MIGNON (RIGHT) The trade name
Mignon was used for dolls made by
Felix Arena of Paris. It is coupled on
this bisque socket head – made in
Germany for Felix Arena – with the
company's mark: a symbol resembling
a biplane or box kite. The mark was
registered in 1918 and was used for the
following two years. Ht: 26in (65cm)

Hands are
molded to
show separate
fingers and
thumbs

Doll's
cotton print
frock is not
original,
but is in
period style

Dress hides
composition legs
and torso, jointed
at knees and hips

Elaborately patterned
knitted wool socks

Ankle-strap
leather shoes,
with ribbon bows

Leather-cloth boots, with
leather soles, originally
belonged to a small child

Leather shoes,
with leather
thong ties

German Marks of Distinction

· 1860s to 1920s ·

THURINGIA BECAME ESTABLISHED as Germany's most important porcelain-producing region from the start of the nineteenth century. Many firms whose main product was porcelain tableware manufactured bisque doll heads and sometimes limbs on behalf of German and French doll-makers that did not have their own porcelain factories, but bought and assembled doll parts, then sold the finished dolls under their own trade name.

Simon and Halbig, established in 1869, was one of these manufacturers. Its production plant and facilities, located at Gräfenhain (near Ohrdruf in Thuringia) were very near the Alt, Beck and Gottschalck factory. Both firms produced many types of high-quality bisque doll heads. Among them were those molded and painted to show highly decorative hairstyles (see pages 44–51).

Jutta doll bodies were manufactured by Cuno and Otto Dressel. The firm's winged helmet mark is stamped in red ink on the doll's right shoulder.

Ears are pierced on the lobes

Curled blond mohair wig, with left-side parting

Molded and painted eyebrows

Bisque socket head, marked on back below hairline

Sleeping violet-blue glass eyes, with top lashes of animal hair

Open mouth, with well-defined, molded top teeth

Composition arms, jointed at elbows, shoulders, and wrists

Base of fingernails is outlined with red paint

Joints at wrists allow hands to rotate

Composition torso, molded as a child's body

Ball joints at hips give legs forward, backward, and sideways movement

Expressively modeled hands have separate fingers and thumbs

Jointed knees; legs can bend backward, but not forward

Composition legs

Doll wears lace-trimmed Swiss cotton dress over two cotton petticoats and baggy knickers

Red paint defines toes and toe-nails

SIMON AND HALBIG HEAD

The bisque socket head, marked with the mold number 1349, identifies this c.1910 doll. The number appears on the dolly face heads that were produced by Simon and Halbig for Cuno and Otto Dressel's Jutta dolls – a line made between 1906 and 1928.

HT: 22in (55cm)

"ANNIE" (ABOVE) This head is incised "905," a mold number used by Simon and Halbig c. 1888 for a range of dolly face swivel heads on shoulder plates. Doll ht: 12in (30cm)

Blond mohair wig

Inset blue glass eyes

Pierced ears

Orange-painted closed mouth

Pale bisque swivel head and shoulder plate

DOLLY FACE (BELOW) "S & H," marked on the back of this doll's bisque socket head, was Simon and Halbig's first trademark, registered in 1905. Ht: 19in (48cm)

Dark blond mohair wig

Inset blue paperweight glass eyes

Closed mouth

SIMON AND HALBIG LOOK-ALIKE (LEFT) Although the bisque socket head of this late 19th-century German doll closely resembles Simon and Halbig heads of the same period, its incised number, 93, does not correspond to any known Simon and Halbig mold. Ht: 23in (58cm)

Clothes conceal a composition body

DOLL MARKS

Many heads look similar, but study of the marks may point to different makers.

Simon and Halbig's Jutta heads bear the doll's name, mold number, size, and trademark.

Alt, Beck and Gottschalck used the number 698 for shoulder heads with cut-out pates.

Brown mohair wig

Sleeping blue glass eyes

Open mouth, with molded top teeth

Double chin and full cheeks are typical dolly face features

Inset brown glass eyes

Wooden arms, jointed at wrists, elbows, and shoulders

Composition hands

Clothing hides composition torso and legs, jointed at hips and knees

Dress of a 1920s bride

Kid shoes and cotton socks

Curly blond mohair wig

Heavily painted, feathered eyebrows

Bisque shoulder head is attached to a stuffed cloth body

POST-1880 ALT, BECK AND GOTTSCHALCK HEAD (ABOVE) The mark incised across the back lower edge of this shoulder head appears to be one used by Alt, Beck and Gottschalck (see Doll Marks, above right). The doll's face is modeled to show the chubby roundness and solemn expression of a young child. Doll ht: 13in (33cm)

SIMON AND HALBIG MOLD NUMBER 905 (RIGHT) Seen from a different angle, the pursed lips of the 905 dolly face are much more evident in this head than in that of "Annie" (see above left). Both dolls have gusseted kid bodies and bisque lower arms. Ht: 17in (43cm)

Straight blond mohair wig over a cork pate

Inset blue-gray glass eyes

Bisque swivel head

Stuffed kid arms, with gussets at elbows

Bisque hands, with short, fat fingers and indented knuckles

Outfit conceals a stuffed kid torso and legs

German Character Dolls

· 1880s to 1900s ·

WHILE MAKERS IN FRANCE continued to create dolls of an almost idealized femininity and beauty, German companies of the late nineteenth century turned their attention toward a novel idea: dolls with facial features modeled on those of real people. Although several manufacturers produced their own versions of these character dolls, as they were called, Kämmer and Reinhardt – founded in 1886 at Waltershausen in Thuringia by doll designer Ernst Kämmer and Franz Reinhardt, a salesman – was the first company to register Character Dolls as a trade name, in 1909.

Kämmer and Reinhardt made only doll bodies, but also produced complete dolls using bisque heads made to its specifications by one of the German porcelain factories. The heads for its character dolls were made by Simon and Halbig (see pages 68–69) and are said to have been modeled on the grandchildren of the company's two founding partners.

Bisque socket head, colored pink to represent a white baby

Molded, painted blond hair

Pale, delicately painted eyebrows

Intaglio eyes, painted pale blue with black pupils

Molded and painted dark brown hair

Intaglio eyes, painted brown

Heavily painted dark eyebrows

Baby mouth, with bowed top lip and droopy lower lip

Mouth is molded into an open smile

Bisque socket head, colored brown to represent a black baby

Deeply creased double chin

Robe conceals a bent-limb, flesh pink composition body, jointed at shoulders and hips

Second and third fingers are molded together; separate thumbs

Bent-limb composition body, jointed at shoulders and hips, painted brown to match coloring of the head

HT: 15in (38cm)

THE BABY *The first of the character dolls to be registered, the Baby head bears the mold number, 100, together with the marks of both Kämmer and Reinhardt and Simon and Halbig. The same mold was used to produce both white and black heads, despite the dissimilar facial characteristics of the ethnic groups that the two colors were intended to represent.*

Black mohair wig

Sleeping brown glass eyes

Open mouth, with molded top teeth

AFRICAN GIRL (LEFT) The Dolls of Four Races were made in Germany between 1890 and 1910, and included European, Oriental, and Indian dolls as well as this African girl. Its Simon and Halbig bisque socket head was a standard dolly face that was "transformed" with the aid of colored glazes, hair, and eyes. Ht: 17in (43cm)

Colored wood and composition body

Miniature, long-haired version of large doll is 5in (13cm) high

Body is jointed at knees, hips, elbows, wrists, and shoulders

Feet are molded to show joined toes, defined with red paint lines

PETER (RIGHT) Heads designed to wear wigs were often given both a boy's and a girl's name. This bisque socket head is a Kämmer and Reinhardt mold number 101, registered in 1909 as Peter and Marie, and made by Simon and Halbig. It has Kämmer and Reinhardt's trademark and the mold number. Ht: 19in (48cm)

First used in 1895, the trademark shows an "&" within a six-point star, flanked by the initials "K" and "R."

Short blond mohair wig

Intaglio eyes, painted brown

Closed mouth

Composition arms, jointed at elbows, wrists, and shoulders

Composition torso, molded to show a child's rotund belly

Composition legs, jointed at knees and hips

Flirty, sleeping glass eyes

Pierced ears

Human hair wig

Open mouth, showing four molded top teeth

Bisque socket head, with mohair wig and inset blue glass eyes

Dress conceals composition body, jointed at shoulders and hips

Lower legs are molded and painted to show stockings and shoes

EUROPEAN GIRL (RIGHT) Designed as one of the Dolls of Four Races (see African Girl above), this dolly face has a Simon and Halbig bisque socket head, and flesh pink, fully jointed composition body. A special attraction is its blue glass eyes, which move from side to side in a flirtatious way. Ht: 17in (43cm)

Painted intaglio eyes

Incised on the nape of the doll's neck, the mold number, registered in 1909, appears directly below the Kämmer and Reinhardt trademark.

ELISE (ABOVE) Mold number 109, called Elise, is one of the rarest of all the Kämmer and Reinhardt character dolls. The head is modeled to show a child's face wearing a rather solemn expression. It has a long mohair wig, styled with a left-side parting and drawn into a bun behind, and intaglio eyes, painted blue-gray. The molded mouth is closed, but deeply indented between its full lips. Doll ht: 19in (48cm)

German Doll-makers

· 1890s to 1930s ·

BY THE END OF THE 1800S, many German factories were involved in the increasingly lucrative doll industry. Some produced only heads, others only bodies; some made the whole doll, and others bought the parts and simply assembled them. A number of these companies started small and expanded gradually. This growth enabled them to produce, assemble, and distribute dolls worldwide.

One such company was Cuno and Otto Dressel of Sonneberg, in Thuringia. Its already established history of trading in dolls and toys had led, by this time, to a flourishing business producing composition doll parts, including heads. Bisque heads were made for the company by leading manufacturers of porcelain, such as Simon and Halbig (see pages 68–69) and Armand Marseille (see pages 76–79).

Large, sleeping glass eyes

Blond mohair wig

Open mouth shows four teeth

Kid upper arms sewn to upper torso

Solid torso made of kid

Lower arms are bisque

Hinged kid thighs allow doll to sit down

Lower legs made of cotton material

Gusseted knees

Separate triangle of cotton forms toes, giving feet some shape

Shoulder head is turned flatteringly to the side

Fashionable dress made of finely pleated silk crepe

Silk damask muff

Elaborate lace trimming on hem, bodice, and sleeves of dress

BISQUE GIRL, "IRENE" *The fine bisque shoulder head of this late 19th-century doll was made by Armand Marseille for Cuno and Otto Dressel. The shoulder plate is marked at the back "COD 93-1 1/2 DEP." Although the doll's body is designed to look natural, it actually bears very little resemblance to the human form.*

HT: 19in (48cm)

Knitted, knee-length stockings

Silk shoes with leather soles

Molded and painted hair

Blue intaglio eyes

Open/closed mouth

Composition body with bent limbs

Bisque socket head

Doll is jointed only at hips and shoulders

The head mark probably dates from 1926.

BABY DOLL (ABOVE) The doll's face and mark resemble those of a Gebrüder Heubach character, but its head was made by Wiefel and Co. Operating from 1912 to the 1930s, this porcelain factory was taken over by Gustav Heubach and Robert Carl in 1926. Ht: 9in (23cm)

J.D. KESTNER DOLLY FACE GIRL (RIGHT) Every company produced its own version of the Dolly Face doll, a universally popular line, along with other, less appealing designs. All these dolls, which could be dressed as girls or boys, have the rounded, slightly double-chinned face of a young child, an open mouth showing teeth, and inset or sleeping eyes. This example has unusual eyes that are brown with a black pupil. Ht: 18½in (47cm)

Dress conceals composition body, jointed at wrists, shoulders, elbows, hips, and knees

C. AND O. DRESSEL LADY WITH ARMAND MARSEILLE HEAD (LEFT) These dolls were first made in 1893. The number 93 (see mark below) was registered by Armand Marseille with C.O.D. in 1892, and probably stands for 1893. A.M. shoulder heads are usually also marked "AM/Made in Germany." Ht: 14½in (37cm)

Silk shoes stamped on leather soles "MADE IN GERMANY"

Blond mohair wig

Sleeping eyes are light blue glass

Open mouth has five teeth

Sleeves conceal cloth upper arms and torso

Bisque lower arms

Beneath dress doll has composition legs, jointed at knees

The mark, incised on the side of the shoulder plate, clearly identifies this particular model.

Bisque socket head with mohair wig

Sleeping eyes are operated by a lead weight

GEBRÜDER HEUBACH DOLLY FACE GIRL (LEFT) This c.1900 doll shows an example of a Dolly Face by another famous maker. With its bisque head and composition body, it looks quite similar to the Kestner version, but this model has sleeping blue glass eyes, and a tongue has been added to create a more realistic effect. Ht: 20in (50cm)

Stylish costume, made c.1920 from racing silks

Silk and lace parasol

Composition hands, jointed at wrists

"Lady Betty Modish"

· 1902 to 1911 ·

THE GERMAN COMPANY J.D. Kestner was founded in 1805 and operated throughout the nineteenth century into the 1930s from its premises in Waltershausen, Thuringia. Its first all-wooden dolls were followed by dolls with composition heads on cloth bodies. By the late 1890s, the company was manufacturing bisque doll heads from its factory in Ohrdruf. ∾ Cooperative trading agreements were common at this time, and many Kestner heads were sold to doll-making firms that did not produce heads of their own. Others were attached to Kestner composition bodies. Completed dolls were exported as far as the United States. Here, fortune smiled on one special doll, and in 1902, "Lady Betty Modish" entered the whirl of fashionable Boston society.

"Gold" metal hair-band, set with pearls and horsehair cockade

Blond human hair wig

Inset brown glass eyes, with finely painted lashes

Open mouth shows four top teeth

Pearl necklace matches the hair ornament

Composition hands, with separate fingers and thumbs

Long blond mohair wig

Bisque dolly face socket head

Wooden disks add strength to jointed parts

Inside body, elastic stringing holds the parts together

Composition arms, jointed at elbows and shoulders

Composition torso, with defined waist and curvy hips

Wooden balls at elbows allow arms to move

Composition upper legs, jointed at hips

Rounded knees and thighs

Composition hands, jointed at wrists

Tops of legs are shaped so that legs can move freely

Wooden balls at knees allow upper and lower legs to move to and fro

Flat feet; red paint detail on molded toes

Shoulders are decorated with satin fabric rosebuds and curled ribbons

Evening gown, made of cream satin, with white net overskirt and low-cut bodice

Satin ribbons and appliquéd flowers, hand-stitched to overskirt

HT: 18in (46cm)

MODEST MISS *The dressed doll at right cuts a fashionable figure, with its lady doll bisque socket head made from mold number 162 and its evening gown, designed and stitched by two Boston ladies. As the gown cannot be taken off, a similar Kestner doll shows the composition body that "Lady Betty Modish" is unable to reveal.*

Satin blouse, with center panel of guipure lace

Purple velvet jacket; sleeves are lined for warmth

Cuffs and collar are trimmed with rabbit fur

VISITING OUTFIT (LEFT) Lavish costumes for all occasions were created for "Lady Betty Modish," despite the doll's attachment to its evening gown. This sumptuous, richly colored ensemble is for winter wear.

Purple velvet-covered cocked hat, with ostrich-feather trim

Inset stiffened lace crown

DOLL MARKS

J.D. Kestner first registered mold numbers for its bisque shoulder and socket heads in 1897.

Incised marks often include "Made in Germany."

Kestner composition bodies have a red ink stamp mark on the torso or buttocks.

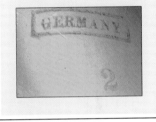

Purple velvet skirt, made in six panels for extra fullness

Pleated cerise silk dust ruffle

52 tiny playing cards: a complete pack

BOUDOIR ACCESSORIES (LEFT AND BELOW) The miniature personal items that "Lady Betty Modish" takes into her "private apartments" are as elegant as any piece of the doll's stylish wardrobe. Still in pristine condition, they are an integral part of this unique collection.

Cream silk stock, secured with a "gold" pin

Brown wool jacket, with nipped-in waist

RIDING HABIT (BELOW) In the early 20th century, hunting was a very popular sport, but no lady would have considered sitting astride a horse. This costume is designed for riding sidesaddle, with a specially cut skirt that permits the merest glimpse of a leather-booted leg.

Knitted woolen riding hose

Loop at top

Nail buffer, with ivory back and chamois pad

Ivory nailbrush, with hair bristles

Dolly's Manicure

Manicure scissors

Metal nail file

Long-sleeved striped silk blouse

Cotton spats, worn over boots

Pearl button fastening

Leather stationery wallet, with writing paper and envelopes

Wool skirt fastens at side with four fabric-covered buttons

Knitting in progress: a lacy bed jacket

Buckled straps go under the feet to keep the spats in place

Metal bag frame, bound with crochet cotton

Silk damask knitting bag

Black and tan leather riding boots, with metal buckles

Armand Marseille Dolls

· 1890s to 1930s ·

BORN IN THE RUSSIAN CITY of St. Petersburg in 1856, Armand Marseille later emigrated with his family to Thuringia in Germany. The region supported a well-established toy- and doll-making industry, which soon captured the young man's interest. In 1885, he bought the porcelain factory of Liebermann and Wegescher in Köppelsdorf and began to manufacture bisque doll heads there five years later. The business went from triumph to triumph. Armand Marseille became one of the largest German manufacturers of bisque doll heads.

Most of the heads made from 1890 to 1920 are the socket type, well cast and finished. The open-mouth, smiling dolly face head of mold number 390 was the most popular. Later heads show a marked deterioration in the quality of the company's workmanship.

Short brown mohair wig, styled in a bowl haircut

Inset dark blue-gray glass eyes

Wig is secured to the head with glue

Bisque socket head, incised "Armand Marseille/Germany/996/A.6.M."

Mouth is molded to show a separate tongue and two top teeth

Enameled golliwog, pinned to wool dickey

Inside torso, arms are strung with elastic from left to right shoulder

Bent arms, made of composition

White silk facings and a collar edged with crocheted cotton

Full sleeves, gathered into narrow cuffs

Composition torso, modeled to show a child's rounded belly and chest

Hands have separate thumbs and fingers

Hip joints allow doll to sit down

Hip-length belt, a popular fashion of the 1920s

Inside torso, legs are strung to head with elastic

Straight, unjointed composition legs, with chubby knees

Long, fine wool coat, with front button fastening

Square feet are flat, with no instep

Indistinctly defined toes

Wool trousers match the coat

LATE 1920S BOY *The mold number, 996, incised on the nape of this doll's neck, appears in the records of Armand Marseille as a baby socket head, with inset or sleeping glass eyes, a molded open/closed mouth, and a wig. Unlike most baby dolls, which feature molded, unjointed bent limbs, this example has straight legs that allow it to stand without support on its flat feet.*

HT: 19in (48cm)

White cotton socks

White kid shoes, tied with purple-red satin ribbon

Bisque socket head, incised "1894/AM 4/ oX DI"

Mohair wig

Closed, pursed-lip mouth

"Germany/ 996/A.3.M." is incised on head

Bisque socket head

DOLL MARKS

Heads are usually incised at the back, below the hairline or on the neck.

~

The mold number and head size appear below the maker's name and country.

TYROLEAN BOY
(ABOVE) *This late 1930s socket head is typical of those produced by Armand Marseille after its boom years. Although the coloring of the head and facial features is quite well done, the finish is rather harsh and considerably less refined than that of earlier heads. Doll ht: 17in (43cm)*

Outfit covers a composition and wood body, jointed at the knees, hips, elbows, and shoulders

Clothes hide composition torso, jointed at hips and shoulders, with straight legs and bent arms

DOLLY FACE GIRL (LEFT) *In the 1930s, this type of doll, with a pretty face and robust, partly jointed composition body, was considered to be an ideal and inexpensive play doll for young children. Ht: 16in (40cm)*

Mohair wig

EARLY 1900S BOY CRICKETER (ABOVE)
Wholesale dolls were often exported and sold unclothed. This dolly face boy's classic cricketing attire — wool shirt and flannels, with a striped blazer and cap — was made by a mother, based on her son's own sporting togs. A tin-box cricket bat completes the outfit. Ht: 14in (35cm)

Mohair wig

Molded eyebrows

Sleeping blue glass eyes

Open mouth has four molded top teeth

Mohair wig

Inset blue glass eyes

Open mouth shows four teeth

FLORODORA (RIGHT) *The trade name Florodora was registered in 1901 for mold number 1374, a bisque socket head. Produced until 1921, many heads were exported to the United States for George Borgfeldt's My Playmate line of dolls. Ht: 16in (40cm)*

C.1900 RED CROSS NURSE (RIGHT) *The familiar dolly face socket head of Armand Marseille mold number 390 is teamed in this doll with an unmarked composition body. Many bodies are so similar in style that it is almost impossible to identify their individual makers if they have no marks. Ht: 16in (40cm)*

Dress conceals fully jointed composition body

The shoe soles are stamped with two German script letters.

My Dream Baby

· 1920s to 1930s ·

UNTIL THE START of the nineteenth century, the word "baby" was used for all dolls, including those representing older children or adults. The very few dolls that were designed to portray babies had neither the facial features nor the body type of their human counterparts, but were simply made shorter than "older" dolls. By 1850, some manufacturers in France and Germany had registered *Bébé* and Baby as trade names, but the dolls so named still resembled young children rather than babies.

In 1909, Kämmer and Reinhardt registered its first character doll baby head (see pages 70–71), along with a special design of bent-limb composition body, and baby dolls began to look like babies. Armand Marseille's mid-1920s version was issued in Germany as My Dream Baby. Heads were sold to other doll producers, including the Averill Manufacturing Co. of New York, which used them for its Lullaby Baby doll line.

Deep, low forehead

Small eyes are set wide apart

Bisque socket head, marked on back "Germany/341/4.K/A.M."

Composition arms, with bent elbows

Red paint lines define joined parts of fingers

Composition torso, modeled as a rounded baby body

Composition legs, molded to show dimpled bent knees

Deep creases between legs and feet

Squat, button nose, with flat bridge

Inside torso, arms are jointed at shoulders with elastic stringing

V-shaped red paint lines between thumbs and first fingers

Inside torso, legs are jointed at hips with elastic stringing

Slightly upturned, stubby feet

Spray-painted, muted color suggests downy hair covering

Softly painted eyebrows

Sleeping blue-gray glass eyes, without lashes

Small, tightly closed mouth

Chubby hands, with separate thumbs and partly joined fingers

Lace trim at sleeve and neck edges

Cream silk baby robe

MOLD NUMBER 341 *Armand Marseille produced more than one style of My Dream Baby. This doll shows the better-quality type. It has a bisque socket head with closed mouth and a bent-limb composition body, designed so that the doll can sit with splayed legs, but not stand.*

HT: 16in (40cm)

Bisque socket head, marked on back "A. M./ Germany/ 351/3.K"

Painted hair, with small curls molded on forehead

Puffy, swollen eye sockets, typical of a newborn baby

Open mouth has two molded bottom teeth

Composition body with bent limbs

Painted hair; no molded detail

Fine brush-strokes indicate eyelashes

Sleeping pale blue-gray glass eyes

DOLL MARKS

Mold number 341 identifies a bisque socket head with closed mouth.

Mold number 351 identifies a bisque socket head with open mouth. "K" for Kurbelkopf indicates a socket head.

CLOSED-MOUTH SOCKET HEAD (ABOVE) Although every head was cast from mold number 341 or 351, the hand-painting of the features makes each one look slightly different. This example, marked "A. M./Germany/341/ 0.K," has the characteristic My Dream Baby face, but with top and bottom lashes painted around the eyes. Doll ht: 12in (30cm)

MOLD NUMBER 351 (ABOVE) Another version of the My Dream Baby bisque socket head, this example shows an open mouth with molded bottom teeth, a design that seems at odds with the concept of a newborn infant. Ht: 12in (30cm)

BLACK BABY (RIGHT) Three other colors of head were issued in addition to the white ones representing Caucasian babies. Described in the words that were used in the 1920s, they are: brown, for "mulatto"; cream, for "Oriental"; and black, for "Negro," shown here. Ht: 24in (60cm)

Molded and painted black hair

Inset very dark brown glass eyes

White bisque socket head, colored brown

Wooden baby rattle, hand-carved in India

Dress conceals slightly bent legs of colored composition, jointed at the hips

Closed-mouth white bisque socket head, colored cream

Original ikat-patterned silk kimono

Inset black glass eyes, with painted lashes

Darker crossline accentuates fullness of lips

Hands, shaped as fists, have separate thumbs

Costume hides a composition body, colored cream

Curved arms, jointed at shoulders, made of colored composition

Broad feet, with poorly defined molded toes

ORIENTAL BABY (ABOVE) Like the black baby, the Oriental head was cast from one of the standard molds used for "white" dolls, with no attempt made at modeling ethnic features. The finger and toe lines, painted orange instead of red, are a special feature. Ht: 9in (23cm)

Bisque Baby Dolls

· 1900s to 1990s ·

THE POPULARITY OF BISQUE-HEADED baby dolls peaked during the 1920s, with the introduction of named models such as George Borgfeldt's Bye-Lo Baby in the United States and Armand Marseille's My Dream Baby in Germany. Many were the product of German manufacturers, whose skilled modeling of character heads satisfied the increasing demand for dolls with realistic features. Designed as newborn infants or older babies, the dolls have heads showing their makers' styles, attached to a common body type. A typical 1920s baby doll has a bisque socket head – most often with molded and painted hair – and a plump composition body. Its unjointed, curved limbs are strung with elastic at the shoulders, so that the arms can move, and at the hips, to allow the doll to sit.

Hair is indicated with feathered brushstrokes

Painted eyebrows

Large ears, molded as one with the head

Human hair lashes, glued into inside top edges of eye sockets

Chin, mouth, and nose are modeled to show deep creases

Open mouth; tongue is molded with bottom lip

Jointed shoulders allow arms to move to and fro

Chubby, curved arms; no elbow joints

Hands have separate thumbs; second and third fingers are molded together

Creases at waist suggest fleshy folds

Composition torso, with rotund belly and rounded chest

Jointed hips allow doll to sit with wide-apart legs

Chubby, curved legs; no knee joints

Feet are modeled to show flexed toes, a typical baby movement

Head is modeled to show the features of a newborn baby

Inset blue glass eyes

Molded top teeth

Traditional christening robe, made of white cotton lawn

Front of robe is edged all around with a border of broderie anglaise

Robe hides period baby undergarments: white cotton undershirt and diaper; cream wool long crossover bodice; and white, lace-trimmed cotton petticoat

MODEL BABY *The finely cast and detailed bisque socket head of this early 20th-century doll is incised "151," a mold number that was registered by several companies, including Hertel, Schwab and Co., to which the head is attributed. The composition body, also of high quality, is a superb example of the bent-limb style that was specially designed for baby dolls.*

HT: 24in (60cm)

Painted eyelashes

Inset blue glass eyes

Small closed mouth

NEWBORN INFANT (LEFT) *This character baby was made by Willy Weyh of Sonneberg in Germany in 1925. It has a bisque flange neck head with a stuffed cloth torso, arms, and legs, and molded composition hands, cast to the wrist joints.*
Ht: 12in (30cm)

The size of the head, 2, appears below the name of the maker as part of the mark.

Clothes hide composition body, jointed at hips and shoulders

Brown human hair wig

Metal eyelids, with hair lashes

Sleeping blue glass eyes

Bisque socket head

The mark incised below the hairline on the back of the head shows the maker's initials and the mold number.

Second and third fingers are joined together, except at tips

Composition bent limbs

Curves of eye sockets are defined with brown paint lines

Painted light blue eyes

Closed mouth, modeled with very full lips

Hand-painted mark below left ear: "LER 92/Tilly/160"

Double chin, a baby doll feature

1992 BABY GIRL, TILLY
(ABOVE) *A traditionally styled doll that brings bisque up to date, Tilly was handcrafted by English doll artists Lynne and Michael Roche. The doll has a bisque flange neck head, with spray-painted hair. Its bent lower arms and legs are also bisque, while the upper limbs and rounded torso are made of firmly stuffed cloth. Ht: 8in (20cm)*

Curved bisque legs, cast to above knee joints

Fine brown paint lines define upper rims of eye sockets

Molded and painted eyes

At back of head, maker's mark reads "FB/0"

Hair is lightly painted in parallel lines

Open/closed mouth

ADVANCED BABY (ABOVE)
Forsaking realism, some makers used wigs to soften the bald heads of their baby dolls, particularly those that were made to portray older children. This c.1916 example is the work of J.D. Kestner. Ht: 18in (46cm)

C.1911 CHARACTER BABY
(LEFT) *Inspired by Kämmer and Reinhardt's first character doll, Baby (see page 70), this model has a bisque socket head made by the German company Fritz Bierschenk. Its bent-limb body is designed as that of a healthy young baby. Ht: 11in (28cm)*

Dress conceals a composition body, jointed at hips and shoulders

Lesser-known German Makers

· 1900s to 1930s ·

AS THE HUB OF THE GERMAN porcelain industry, Thuringia supported numerous small doll-makers as well as the factories that manufactured doll heads for large companies. The work of these lesser-known makers has often survived not because the dolls are of superior quality, but simply because they were made in great numbers. Considered playthings to be thrown away when broken, very large quantities were produced. Even the businesses of smaller makers were sustained by the public demand for such dolls.

These two pages show the work of less celebrated German makers. Each doll has a bisque head incised with the marks of a known and recognized manufacturer. Finding identifiable marks is a stroke of luck, as many makers did not mark their products.

Titian mohair or human hair wig

Painted top and bottom eyelashes

Sleeping blue glass eyes

Ears are pierced for earrings

Sleeping eyes, with metal lids, in half-closed position

Open mouth, showing four top teeth

Simon and Halbig bisque socket head, marked on back "79/10/Germany/HANDWERCK"

Separate thumbs and spread fingers

Composition arms, jointed at elbows, shoulders, and wrists

Composition torso, molded to show a child's pronounced belly and small chest

Red paint lines define finger-nail ridges

Arms are painted flesh pink

Cotton lawn dress, trimmed with satin ribbon, lace, and broderie anglaise

Composition upper legs, shaped at tops of thighs so doll can sit easily

Wooden balls give upper and lower legs easy movement

Composition lower legs, with curved calves

Painted red toe and toenail detail

Chubby, creased ankles

HEINRICH HANDWERCK

Founded in 1855 as a toy-making company, Heinrich Handwerck later switched to composition doll bodies, which were attached to Handwerck-designed Simon and Halbig bisque heads. This finely modeled c.1900 dolly face girl typifies one of the most popular styles of the period.

Color coordinated cotton socks

Pigskin shoes, with metal buckles

HT: 19in (48cm)

The mark, incised on the back of the head, also includes "Germany/4" below the designer-maker's name. Max Handwerck operated in Waltershausen from 1900 until the 1930s.

Composition body, jointed at shoulders, elbows, wrists, hips, and knees

MAX HANDWERCK, GIRL

(ABOVE) *The composition doll bodies made by this company were teamed with one of two types of bisque head, many of which were produced in the porcelain factory of William Goebel. Socket heads, like this one, came with sleeping glass eyes and mohair wigs. Shoulder heads were usually finished with molded and painted hair and painted eyes. Doll ht: 27in (68cm)*

The Hermann Steiner mark shows an "H" entwined with "St."; size number is below.

HERMANN STEINER, DOLLY FACE

(RIGHT) *In 1920, bisque doll heads joined the stuffed plush animals that had been Hermann Steiner's stock-in-trade since the establishment of the company in Neustadt in 1911. This example, made in the 1920s, has a composition torso and fully jointed wooden limbs. Steiner still produces toys but not dolls. Ht: 17in (43cm)*

Blond mohair wig

Inset brown glass eyes

Open mouth, with four top teeth

Bisque socket head

Hands jointed at wrists

Blond mohair wig, on a bisque socket head

Sleeping blue glass eyes, with hair lashes

C.1925 GIRL

(RIGHT) *Arthur Schoenau and Carl Hoffmeister had already proved their ability as doll-makers when they joined forces in 1901 to form the Schoenau and Hoffmeister Porzellanfabrik Burggrub. The company produced its bisque doll heads — of which this is a good example — in its own porcelain factory. Ht: 28in (70cm)*

Dress hides a fully jointed composition torso and limbs

The incised mark shows the initials of the factory name above the size and mold numbers.

Boots hide wooden legs, with very long thighs, jointed at knees and hips

Reddish brown coarse mohair wig

Sleeping googly blue glass eyes

Bisque socket head

Bisque arms, jointed at shoulders

J. WALTHER AND SOHN, C.1920 GOOGLY-EYED DOLL

(RIGHT) *The charming bisque character head of this doll was made in the Oeslau, Coburg, porcelain factory of Johann Walther. It is incised on the back with the crown symbol of the firm, together with "W & S" entwined. Ht: 7in (18cm)*

Dress hides composition legs and torso; lower legs have molded and painted shoes and stockings

Ethnic and English Dolls

· 1860s to 1920s ·

THE STORY OF DOLLS and their makers has linked numerous countries not only through mutually beneficial trade and enterprise, but also as a result of historical events. Some of the most interesting and unusual dolls have been made during periods of conflict, or as designers tried to create new and exciting models that would spark the imagination of the buying public and – in so doing – loosen its purse strings. For many collectors, dolls of this kind have a very special charm that balances their sometimes idiosyncratic appearance.
All the dolls described on these two pages illustrate how English and German manufacturers reacted to changes in their familiar worlds during the second half of the nineteenth century and the first two decades of the twentieth century – changes that led, on one hand, to broadened horizons and, on the other, to newly entrenched and insular attitudes.

Slanted, curved eyebrows: the only "realistic" facial feature

Closed mouth

Silk-covered cardboard hat has a braided silk trim

Pierced ears: a common feature of late 19th-century German doll heads

Tinted bisque socket head

Elbow-length sleeves are lined with pink silk

Incised under hair, "220": the mold number for an Oriental head, registered in 1888

Mohair wig, braided into a long pigtail

Hands have separate thumbs and joined fingers

Composition arms, jointed at shoulders

Back of jacket shows its original olive green color

Front of silk jacket has faded from its original olive green color to dun brown

Woven silk damask underskirt

Clothes hide composition legs, jointed at knees and hips and strung to a composition torso

Split-sided tunic coat, made of dark blue silk

Pink wool is braided in with the pigtail and secures its end

Linen hose, with woven patterning

Small feet evoke the Chinese custom of foot-binding

Pink silk also lines the body of the coat

MANDARIN'S SON *Ethnic dolls became popular in the late 19th century, when new possibilities for world travel brought an awareness of other cultures to the masses. Companies that added such dolls to their product line used standard molds not modified to show realistically ethnic features. This doll's bisque socket head, made in Germany by Bähr and Pröschild, hardly resembles the Chinese boy that it is meant to portray.*

HT: 12in (30cm)

Composition lower legs, molded and painted to show Chinese-style slippers and socks

Black astrakhan wig

Inset very dark brown glass eyes

Standard bisque dolly face socket head, with applied color

Open mouth, painted orange, with three molded top teeth

Slightly curved composition arms

Beneath jerkin, arms are jointed at shoulders

Coral pink satin jerkin, embroidered with gold braid

Hands are coarsely modeled, with joined fingers and separate thumbs

Clothes conceal the tinted composition torso

Cotton muslin dhoti: a type of one-piece pants

Feet are crudely modeled, with ill-defined toes

1860s Doll in Indian State Costume (RIGHT)
A glazed china head with an elaborately molded hairstyle has been used for this unusual doll, which represents a male court official in Raipur, India, at the turn of the century. Originally designed to show the features of a girl, the face has been painted with a fine set of sideburns and a curled mustache. Ht: 22in (55cm)

Inset blue glass eyes

Pierced ears, hung with ornate earrings

Sleeves hide bisque arms, jointed at the shoulders

Very finely modeled hands

Clothes conceal bisque legs, jointed at hips to a stuffed cloth torso

Magnificent costume, made of linen, silk, and muslin

Slender fingers and thumbs

Gold anklets

Tiny feet, molded and painted to show heeled, gaiter-type boots

RUNNING FOOTMAN (ABOVE)
The bisque socket head of this doll bears a raised mark similar to some of those used by Walther and Co., a company that produced doll heads in its own porcelain factory from 1908. The doll itself is thought to represent an Eygptian servant. Its head and composition body are tinted to show the tones of a dark-skinned man. Ht: 11in (28cm)

Stuffed cloth upper arms

Stoneware lower arms

Elongated, firmly stuffed torso

Stuffed cloth upper legs

Painted intaglio eyes

Legs swivel at hips, but shape of torso hinders sitting position

Open/closed mouth, with molded tongue and top teeth

Stoneware lower legs

ENGLISH BABY (RIGHT)
During World War I, supplies of imported German dolls were withdrawn from sale in Great Britain, yet buyers still wanted bisque-headed dolls. This doll illustrates a typical example of the stoneware heads that were produced by some English porcelain factories to fill the gap in the market. Ht: 20in (50cm)

Molded and painted hair

The mark incised on the back of the head includes "H" and "L," for Hewitt and Leadbeater.

WILLOW POTTERY, BABY HEAD (LEFT)
English pottery company Hewitt and Leadbeater manufactured Willow Pottery stoneware doll heads from 1914 to 1920. This shoulder head shows one of its many styles. Doll ht: 14in (35cm)

Mass-produced Bisque Dolls

· 1900s to 1940s ·

IN THE LATE NINETEENTH and early twentieth centuries, France and Germany cornered the market for bisque dolls. The glazed china and untinted bisque heads with elaborately molded hairstyles, prim-faced lady dolls in gorgeous attire, and character dolls of this period are some of the finest examples of doll-making. But after 1900, and particularly between World Wars I and II, new possibilities for world trade opened up, and encouraged the mass production of inexpensive dolls, as forward-looking manufacturers capitalized on an increasingly lucrative export market.

∿ Such dolls are often of the "cheap and cheerful" variety. Many were produced to be sold at fairs and in amusement parks, or as vacation souvenirs; some were made as ornamental pieces, aimed more toward adult than child buyers, and can hardly be thought of as play dolls; others originated as fictional characters.

The designer's surname appears as a signature, impressed into the base of both feet.

Long wisps of hair, painted from knob on crown to forehead

Top of head is molded and painted to show a knob of hair

Single molded and painted knob of hair on either side of head

Tiny molded wings, painted blue, a special Kewpie feature

Large eyes, painted in the typically side-glancing position

Hair is painted in wispy brushstrokes at nape of neck

Molded, tiny button nose

Mouth is a single molded and painted line, set in a broad smile

Shoulder joints have metal pins that allow arms to move

Printed paper label shows the Kewpie trade name, registered by George Borgfeldt in 1913, and the doll's country of origin

All-bisque arms

All-bisque body, molded as one with the head

"Starfish" hands, a typical Kewpie feature

Hands are molded to show separate thumbs and spread, slightly "webbed," fingers

Diminutive rump; paintwork accentuates each tiny buttock

Molded belly button, tinted with rosy pink highlights

Molded legs are joined together

Short, stubby feet

Depressions between ankles and thighs give shape to backs of legs

Legs are modeled to show a young child's chubby thighs

Tinges of darker color define "hipline" at base of torso

Splotches of color suggest knees

Narrow grooves give definition to the molded, joined toes

ALL-BISQUE KEWPIE *Based on illustrations by Rose O'Neill in* Ladies' Home Journal *and elsewhere, the original Kewpies were modeled by Joseph Kallus and produced by George Borgfeldt, a company in New York where Mr Kallus worked as a designer. This doll is one of the earliest models, which were made in the porcelain factory of German doll manufacturer J.D. Kestner.*

HT: 7in (18cm)

Molded and painted hair

Coarsely modeled facial features

Bisque shoulder head

Dumpy bisque lower arms

Well-modeled hair

Stuffed cloth upper arms

Bisque lower legs

Stuffed cloth upper legs and torso

Jester's hat is molded as part of the head

Arms are pinned to shoulders with bent-ended wires

Plump cheeks, painted to show a florid complexion

Paint highlights costume details

Lower arms are molded as gauntlets

Hips are strung with elastic

Lower legs are molded to show wide trouser hems

Stiffened canvas hat, with braid trim and wool flowers

Mohair wig

Painted facial features

Ceramic arms, jointed at shoulders

Ceramic legs, jointed at hips

Lower legs are painted to show boots

1920S CARNIVAL KEEPSAKE
(ABOVE) Made in Germany, this all-bisque figure has a one-piece head and torso, molded and painted to show a jester's costume. Crude joints at the shoulders and hips allow the limbs to swing when the doll is jiggled. Ht: 2½in (6cm)

Bisque lower legs, painted to show shoes

1930S HOLIDAY
SOUVENIR (RIGHT) Though wearing the regional costume of Alsace in France, this doll is probably of German origin. Its head and torso, cast as a single unit, and unjointed limbs are all made of a low-grade ceramic material. Ht: 4in (10cm)

JAPANESE DOLLS (ABOVE)
When Germany suspended the production of bisque dolls during World War I, the United States turned to Japan for supplies. This pair shows the poor quality of Japanese dolls made for export. Ht: Boy 7in (18cm); girl 6in (15cm)

RECLINING LADIES (RIGHT)
High-quality bisque figurines were popular ornaments between 1900 and 1930, their willowy, nude – or seminude – bodies gracing many a boudoir dressing table or mantelpiece. These two naturists, made in Germany c.1920, are unusually adorned with mohair wigs. Ht: 5in (13cm)

Gracefully angled head

Strawberry blond mohair wig; molded hair is more typical

Eyes and brows are delicately painted

Body is modeled to show a slim, curvy torso and slender limbs

Recumbent figures are the most often seen type

Body is fixed into an alluring "come-hither" position

Molded and painted hair

Well-modeled eyes, nose, and open/closed mouth

Wired joints at shoulders

Legs are jointed to one-piece torso and head with elastic stringing

1930S GERMAN BISQUE
BABIES (ABOVE) Inexpensively made in large numbers, small bisque dolls like these found a ready market among children as dolls' house figures. Many came fully clothed in pastel-colored crocheted garments. Ht: Largest 3in (7.5cm); smallest 1½in (4cm)

Feet are molded and painted to show slippers

Printed Cloth Dolls

· 1900s to 1980s ·

AS DEMAND FOR COMMERCIALLY made rag dolls increased, factories began to produce printed cloth dolls, sometimes known as cut-out cloth dolls. The front and back of each doll were printed onto cotton sheets. Then the sheet of cloth would be sold, ready to be cut out, sewn together, and stuffed with kapok, straw, or even sawdust by the buyer. These dolls represented a variety of characters – some were well known, such as a celebrity or storybook character; others represented types, such as a pretty girl or soldier.

Although the first printed cloth dolls were made in the last half of the nineteenth century, most of the dolls that survive were manufactured after 1900. The chromolithographic process caused the fabric to deteriorate, as did rough handling and washing; in some cases, the stuffing was eaten away by animals or insects.

Doll's name is printed on cap

Idealized features: "rosebud" mouth and large eyes

Patriotic stars and stripes on cap and T-shirt

Outfit represents the Liberty Bell in Philadelphia

Hanging loop attached at shoulder seams

Liberty Bell's crack reproduced on doll

Company name printed at base of bell

Printed cloth label shows limited-edition number (891)

All-in-one cloth body stuffed with kapok

MISS LIBERTY BELLE *Produced in 1976, this doll commemorates 200 years of American independence on the front of her dress, and 150 years of independence on the back. It is named after the Liberty Bell in Philadelphia, Pennsylvania. Printed by the Toy Works (Hodge Podge) in Massachusetts, it is a limited-edition doll.*

HT: 14½in (36.5cm)

Distinctive ponytail

Printed cloth body, prestuffed with kapok

"Tails" give an extra dimension to the doll

Cereal package features Sunny Jim character

RED RIDING HOOD
(RIGHT) This cut-out doll pattern was printed in the United States c. 1970. For economic reasons, cut-out doll patterns were usually printed continuously onto a large piece of cloth, which was then sold by the yard (or meter). These shapes were printed on a cotton strip 18in (46cm) wide. Ht: 16½in (42cm)

Red cape is a separate cut-out shape

Design shows how doll should look after sewing

Front and back of doll to be stuffed and sewn up

Red kerchief

SUNNY JIM (LEFT) In 1905, A.C.
Fincken, the manufacturer of Force Wheat Flakes, a breakfast cereal launched in 1901 in the United States, issued a printed cloth doll to promote its product. Sunny Jim, a caricature of an early 1800s gentleman, could be obtained by sending coupons and a small sum of money to the manufacturer. Both Force Wheat Flakes and the doll are still available today. This model dates from c. 1970. Ht: 16in (41cm)

Yellow and beige wool sewn onto head

Facial features printed onto cloth

STRUWWELPETER (RIGHT) This well-
known German storybook character, Struwwelpeter ("Shock-headed Peter"), was the creation of Dr. Heinrich Hoffmann. Since the publication of Hoffmann's cautionary tales in 1845, Struwwelpeter, the disobedient boy who refused to cut his hair or nails, has been portrayed in doll form many times. This printed cloth model was made in the Far East. Ht: 13in (33cm)

Fronts and backs of all four dolls printed on single sheet

Clothes based on the storybook illustration

PRINTED DOLLS
(LEFT) Printed onto a cotton sheet, the dolls are named Cora, Agnes, Sylvia, and May. They were designed by Samuel Finburgh and first printed in 1916. In the 1970s the designs were reprinted by Hulbert Fabrics A.U.L. for Her Majesty's Stationery Office, which supplied them to the Bethnal Green Museum of Childhood in London. Ht: 15½in (39cm)

Nails 1in (2.5cm) long are made of vinyl and glued onto cloth hands

Printed label indicates doll is copyright of Heinrich-Hoffmann-Museum GmbH

~ Steiff Dolls ~

· 1900s to the present day ·

THE STEIFF COMPANY, established by Margarete Steiff in 1877, is still in business today. Although probably best known for its teddy bears, it also produced a wide range of dolls and other stuffed toys. These two pages show a selection of Steiff rag dolls made in the early 1900s. Steiff dolls of this period were usually made of felt, and the range of characters they portrayed was diverse. Many were caricatures of types, such as policemen, circus entertainers, or sailors, with exaggerated and often comical features. Some represented storybook characters.

~ Distinguishing features of Steiff dolls include a center or diagonal seam on the face, and the company's "Button-in-Ear" trademark (see Doll Marks, opposite). If the button is missing from the doll, there are usually telltale signs where it was once punched through the felt.

Shiny black shoe-button eyes sewn into face

Smile indicated with red paint

Limp gray mohair sewn to head

Socket head, made of molded felt

Unpainted cloth body, jointed at shoulders

Posture of old woman: drooping bustline, sagging stomach, and rounded shoulders

Jointed hips allow some movement

Thumb is separate from fingers, but cut from the same piece of cloth

Large hands appear rather swollen

Knees are fixed in a bent position

Large feet; no toes

HT: 19in (48cm)

OLD WOMAN *First marketed in 1913, this doll was reissued in the late 1980s. It is an unusually life-like portrayal of an elderly woman with sagging posture. The legs are the most startling feature: bent and gnarled, they even show traces of varicose veins.*

Wide mouth is stitched and painted red

Curly white mohair plush hair extends around the back of the head

Shirt decorated with red bow tie at neck and small black buttons

Blue felt suit trimmed with ribbed brass buttons

Large, round felt patches represent spectacles

Back of Steiff button is visible in left ear

Black shoe-button eyes sewn onto felt spectacles

HEAD DETAIL (ABOVE) Available between 1905 and 1914, this all-felt doll bears a Steiff metal button in its ear (see Doll Marks, right). These buttons were usually attached to the doll's left ear and could face either forward or backward.

DOLL MARKS

"Button-in-Ear" was registered as a trademark in May 1905.

~

Dolls made after 1905 bear a metal button marked "STEIFF" in raised lettering (see below).

~

In 1908–1909 a cloth label, printed with the product number, was attached to the metal button.

~

From 1926 a chest label was added to Steiff dolls.

Hands in clenched fist position, fingers indicated by stitching

GROSSPAPA (LEFT) With his white hair and knobby knees, Grosspapa (or Grandpapa) clearly represents an elderly man. His upright posture and clenched fists indicate that he is a proud and robust character. Ht: 14½in (37cm)

Felt legs are also intended to be trousers

Long, pointed shoes, worn with felt spats, are made of brown leather

Blond mohair plush hair, sewn onto head and clipped short

Nostrils are painted red for realistic effect

Lips and flesh tones are tinted soft red

Green felt suspenders, embroidered with yellow chainstitching

Fingers indicated by beige mercerized cotton thread

Shaped fingers and thumbs

Characteristic Steiff seam down center of face

Seams on either side of the eyes give doll interesting expression

"Button-in-Ear" faces backward

Lips made of a separate piece of felt sewn in and painted

Felt breeches, trimmed with chainstitch, are tied at knee

"GEORGE" (LEFT) Steiff's trade name for this model was actually Hans, but this particular doll was renamed "George" by its owner. An all-felt construction, the doll is similar to Anthony (right), but twice the size. Ht: 24in (60cm)

ANTHONY (LEFT) Made by Steiff in 1909, Anthony was distributed by Borgfeldt in the United States. It was available in five sizes, from 11in (28cm) to 24in (60cm); some models contained a voice box in the torso. The traditional Tyrolean costume is completely original, and made of good-quality materials. Ht: 11in (28cm)

English Manufacturers

· 1920s to 1950s ·

BETWEEN 1920 AND 1940, RAG DOLLS enjoyed a new wave of popularity. Working at the same time as Lenci in Italy and Käthe Kruse in Germany (see pages 100–101), English companies produced many new models of rag dolls in quantity for the domestic and international markets. These represented a wide range of character types. Often they were made as souvenirs, portraying a famous figure such as a new king. One of the most successful English companies to make rag dolls was Chad Valley Co. Ltd. Originally a printing firm called Johnson Brothers, it was established c.1850 in Birmingham. The firm was renamed Chad Valley in 1897, and diversified to manufacture games, jigsaw puzzles, and stuffed toys. The first dolls were produced c.1920.

The label, tied to the right wrist, indicates that the doll is safe for children.

Reddish brown mohair is sewn on to form a side part

Facial features molded from stiffened felt and painted

Socket head is made of firmly stuffed felt

Cotton dress is part of the doll's structure and cannot be removed

Kapok-stuffed calico body, jointed at shoulders and hips

American-cloth trim on cuffs and collar

Velvet arms, covered by the cotton uniform

Separate, but not applied, thumb

Hygienic Toys label attached to right wrist

Hands are stitched to indicate fingers

Shiny black American-cloth shoes

Cotton stockings conceal velvet legs

CHAD VALLEY CO. LTD., NURSE *A fine example of a Chad Valley doll, this model was first issued c.1930. The Hygienic Toys/Seal of Purity label indicates that this model is made of safe, good-quality materials. It distinguishes the doll from many Eastern European imports made during this period, which contained sawdust, moss, or animal hair.*

HT: 19½in (48.5cm)

DEAN'S RAG BOOK CO. LTD., LUPINO LANE (LEFT)

The wire-frame base, covered with padding, is completely flexible and allows the limbs of this 1939 doll to be bent into different positions. Lupino Lane was the star of the musical Me and My Girl. *Ht: 12½in (31.5cm)*

This printed label is attached to the sole of the doll's right foot.

Label indicates actor's name and song from the musical

Woolen checked suit is part of body structure

Doll's limbs are completely flexible

J.K. FARNELL AND CO. LTD., H.M. THE KING (RIGHT)

J.K. Farnell was established as a toy-maker c.1870 in Acton, London, and began producing dolls in 1915. This doll, made in 1937, commemorated the coronation of George VI, after the abdication of his brother, Edward VIII. *Ht: 15in (38cm)*

The label is attached under the doll's right pocket flap.

"Sleepy" features painted onto molded felt face

SLEEPY

Black teased-wool bearskin, with 2in- (5cm) high woolen plume

Facial features molded from stiffened felt and painted

Costume is replica of Royal Highlanders' uniform

Metal sword painted black with gold tip

White plush sporran with black braid tassels

A label, attached to the sole of the foot, bears the name of the manufacturer

HAPPY

CHAD VALLEY CO. LTD., SEVEN DWARFS (BELOW)

In 1937, Walt Disney released its animated cartoon Snow White and the Seven Dwarfs. In 1938, Chad Valley produced the characters from the cartoon in doll form. The faces are individually molded from felt and painted, giving each dwarf a unique facial expression and personality. *Ht: 6½in (16.5cm)*
© The Walt Disney Company

MERRYTHOUGHT LTD., HAPPY AND SLEEPY (ABOVE and RIGHT)

Merrythought was founded in 1930, and is still in business to this day. In the mid-1950s, the firm made a set of Walt Disney's Snow White and the Seven Dwarfs. *Ht: 10in (24.5cm)*
© The Walt Disney Company

Fingers indicated with stitching; separate, but not applied, thumb

A woven label, concealed by the jacket, is sewn to the body of each dwarf shown below.

SNEEZY SLEEPY DOPEY GRUMPY BASHFUL DOC HAPPY

Trousers are part of the legs   *Removable felt jackets*   *Pink cotton bodies and backs of heads*   *Label reads, "THIS IS HAPPY"*

European Manufacturers

· 1920s to 1950s ·

BY THE 1920s, several European manufacturers were producing very high-quality rag dolls. Sometimes known as "art dolls," these were often designed and painted by talented artists, and modeled by highly skilled craftsmen. German doll-maker Käthe Kruse and the Italian firm Lenci were two of the leading manufacturers of rag dolls. Both of these companies are still in business.

Käthe Kruse, wife of sculptor Max Kruse, was a talented painter; she began making dolls c.1911. Convinced that bisque dolls were not practical toys, she decided that her dolls would be unbreakable and easy to play with. Lenci was founded in Turin in 1918 by Elena Scavini. It is thought that she named the firm after her own pet name, Lenci.

Side-glancing, painted brown eyes, with black pupils

Nostrils are painted in red

Typical Lenci mouth is closed and painted in red

Reddish blond mohair is sewn onto head

Boyish features are molded and painted

Separate, shaped ears

Socket head made of stiffened felt

Two fingers are joined on hand; typical Lenci feature

Smock was made at same time as doll

Torso, like the head, is made of stiffened and molded felt

Joints at shoulders and hips allow some movement

Piglet is a 1950s copy of the toy made for author A.A. Milne's son, the original Christopher Robin

LENCI, BOY *Made in the 1920s, this is a fine example of a Lenci doll. Although it bears a remarkable resemblance to E.H. Shepard's illustrations of Christopher Robin, the hero of A.A. Milne's famous Pooh Bear stories, there is no evidence to suggest that Lenci modeled the doll on this character. It is extremely lifelike, and has a charming, slightly wary expression.*

HT: 19in (47.5cm)

LENCI, BELLBOY (LEFT) This bellboy character, made by Lenci c. 1920, was available as a black or white doll. The number identifies this doll as a fairly early Lenci model: the model numbers began with 100 and passed 2000 by 1930. The small button attached to the bellboy's cuff is the first style of Lenci button produced. Ht: 11in (28cm)

Black plush hair, sewn on

Molded bulbous eyes; right eye is partly closed

Shaped fingers and thumbs; stitching indicates gloves

Raised, molded button attached to left cuff reads "Lenci"

Red felt suit

Black oilcloth shoes, with white felt spats

LENCI, GIRL (LEFT) This c. 1922 doll has typical Lenci features: brown painted eyes looking to the side, a small, rosebud mouth, and a rather sullen expression. Lenci designs are very distinctive; however, the untagged dolls are often quite difficult to identify, as other manufacturers tended to imitate many of the company's designs. Ht: 12½in (32cm)

Highlights painted in white onto iris

All-in-one cotton and lace undergarment

Original cream felt dress, trimmed with dark turquoise felt

Fingers are indicated by stitches; separate thumb, but cut from same piece of fabric

This metal button, attached to the doll's undergarment, is the second style of Lenci button produced.

MAGDA BOALT, SWEDISH DOLL (RIGHT) Sometimes known as the Swedish Käthe Kruse, Magda Boalt is probably Scandinavia's best-known doll-maker. A one-time hairdresser, she began by making small wigs for dolls, using remnants of human hair. In 1944, she made her first doll. This model was manufactured c. 1950. Ht: 19in (48cm)

Molded and painted face intended to resemble that of a child as closely as possible

Dress conceals cloth body and limbs, stuffed with a soft but hard-wearing filling

Human hair wig; hairs are sewn onto a thin silk skullcap, three at a time

Black leather shoes, with metal buckles

KÄTHE KRUSE, BABY (RIGHT) It is said that Käthe Kruse made her first doll from a potato and a towel filled with sand. By 1911, she was producing high-quality rag dolls in quantity. The construction of this 1920s baby doll is complicated; it has been assembled from numerous panels of cloth, which have been sewn together. Ht: 16in (41cm)

Characteristic three seam lines at back of head

C-shaped ears applied to head separately

Wrist originally bore a label with doll's name

Body has two seams at front and back; five-panel leg construction

Foot is lined with stiff paper and stamped with product number

Norah Wellings

· 1919 to 1960 ·

NORAH WELLINGS BEGAN HER CAREER in 1919 with the Chad Valley Co. Ltd. (see pages 98–99). In 1926, she opened her own factory, Victoria Toy Works, in Shropshire, England, where she designed and made dolls until 1960. During this time, she also designed dolls for Chad Valley. For this reason, many dolls produced by these two firms are quite similar. However, those manufactured at the Norah Wellings factory can be identified by a woven label sewn to the body (see Doll Marks, opposite).

Norah Wellings dolls are generally made of felt, velvet, and velveteen, and represent children and adults. She produced many ethnic dolls as well as numerous storybook characters. Probably the finest Norah Wellings dolls were made in the 1930s.

Heart-shaped face molded from stiffened felt

Side-glancing blue eyes, painted in oil colors

Two red painted dots accentuate the nostrils

Reddish brown mohair is sewn to head

Swivel head is turned to side

Orange, peasant-style felt dress with laced bodice

Shoulder joints allow some movement

Original wooden-bead bracelets, attached to both wrists, cannot be removed

Only two fingers sewn together, an unusual feature

Jointed at hips to allow movement

Legs are shaped to define calves and ankles

Toes indicated by stitching; label sewn to base of left foot

Orange felt shoes, with metal buttons

ORANGE GIRL *This large, 1930s felt doll has a swivel head. The body is stuffed and jointed at the shoulders and hips, and the facial features are molded and painted. The hands are of special interest, as only two of the fingers are joined together. Usually, the fingers of Norah Wellings dolls are indicated by stitching, with a separate thumb.*

HT: 17½in (44cm)

SAILORS (LEFT) These c.1928
dolls were sold on board passenger
liners as souvenirs. They were made
in two styles: "grinning" sailors
(top), with felt feet and large,
protruding, pointed ears; and
"smiling" sailors (bottom),
with velvet feet and flat
ears. Ht: 8½in (21cm)

*Hat, stamped
with name of ship*

*Woven label, sewn
to sole of left foot*

HARRY THE HAWK (BELOW)
During World War II, Norah
Wellings made dolls representing
characters from the Army, Royal
Navy, and Royal Air Force. This
mascot doll, Harry the Hawk, raised
funds for men serving in the Royal
Air Force (R.A.F.) during the war.
Ht: 7in (18cm)

*Felt parachute, in
patriotic colors*

DOLL MARKS
Sewn-on cloth labels were
firmly stitched to Norah
Wellings dolls.

The labels are black, blue,
or beige, depending on the
color of the doll.

MADE IN ENGLAND
BY
NORAH WELLINGS

Labels are usually sewn to
the foot, but can appear on
the wrist or on the doll's back.

MADE IN ENGLAND
BY
NORAH WELLINGS

*Felt flowers
worn in hair*

ORIENTAL GIRL (LEFT) This
1930s all-felt doll is not merely a
standard model dressed in
oriental clothing. The face has
been carefully designed to
portray specific ethnic
characteristics; the coloring is
as true to life as possible. A
Norah Wellings label is sewn
to the foot. Ht: 12½in (31cm)

*Fingers are indicated
by stitching;
separate thumb*

*Felt Japanese-
style kimono*

*Woven label sewn
to sole of right foot*

*Brown felt intended
to represent leather
gauntlets*

*Outfit is based on
authentic R.A.F.
flying combat
coveralls*

*Label indicates that
the R.A.F. benefits
from sales of the doll*

*Colored-velvet
uniforms are part
of doll's body*

GUARDSMEN (RIGHT) Like the sailors
shown above, two styles of guardsmen
dolls were available: those that grin,
and those that smile. Both wear the
same uniform, and were made in a
range of sizes, some as large as 36in
(91cm). These models were made in
the 1930s. Ht: Largest 33½in
(84.5cm); smallest 10in (25cm)

German Manufacturers

· 1870s to 1960s ·

ESTABLISHED IN BAVARIA in 1873 by Friedrich Bensinger, the Rheinische Gummi- und Celluloid-Fabrik was the major producer of celluloid in Germany. Today, the company produces vinyl dolls from its original factory in Mannheim–Neckarau; since the early 1950s, it has operated under the name Schildkröt-Spielwaren GmbH. *Schildkröte* is the German word for "turtle," and the company's main trademark was a walking turtle encased in a diamond, which was molded on the doll necks and bodies. The mark is raised. In some cases the diamond is omitted, or the turtle is enclosed in a circle, square, oval, triangle, or hexagon. Other manufacturers of celluloid also used the trademark of a turtle to represent durability; however, the raised turtle-in-a-diamond was exclusive to the Rheinische Gummi- und Celluloid-Fabrik.

The turtle mark and model number and signature of Käthe Kruse appear on the back of the doll.

Inset blue glass eyes

Molded nose; nostrils painted in red

Molded and painted brown hair

Eyebrows are painted in brown

Dress has small orange-red bow at neck of cape collar

Head and torso molded as one; head cannot turn

Celluloid body, jointed at shoulders

Straight arms are shaped to define elbows

Blue cotton dress conceals white one-piece undergarment

Molded fingers, with separate thumbs

Jointed hips allow some movement

Straight legs are shaped to define knees

Feet point inward; molded toes

Wrist tag, with turtle-in-a-diamond trademark

Cream machine-knitted socks

Red leather shoes with metal buckles

KÄTHE KRUSE, BLUE-DRESS GIRL *In the mid-1950s, Käthe Kruse worked with the Rheinische Gummi- und Celluloid-Fabrik to produce all-celluloid dolls, and dolls made of Tortulon — a new plastic that resembled hard vinyl. This model is made entirely of celluloid, yet manages to retain the facial characteristics of a Käthe Kruse rag doll (see pages 100–101).*

HT: 14in (35cm)

BUSCHOW AND BECK, BOY

(RIGHT) Buschow and Beck, famous for its doll heads, was founded in Silesia, Germany, in 1888. This figure, made in the 1920s, has a celluloid head and cloth body, and may be a Käthe Kruse design. Ht: 12in (30cm)

Molded hair, painted brown

Celluloid socket head can turn

Cloth torso, jointed at shoulders

The head mark bears the helmet trademark, mold number, and size number.

Joints at hips and shoulders allow some movement of limbs

Cloth limbs, stuffed with excelsior

Feet are made from separate piece of fabric

Toes are indicated by stitching

MADAME HENDREN, BOY

(RIGHT) Madame Hendren was the trade name used between 1915 and 1965 for dolls that were designed and patented by Madame Georgene Averill and made by the Averill Manufacturing Co. of New York City. Ht: 18in (46cm)

Oddly shaped, irregular teeth

Celluloid head is molded with turtle-in-a-diamond mark on the back

Peach cotton smock conceals cloth body

The cloth body is stamped "GENUINE 'MADAME HENDREN' DOLL/1920/ MADE IN U.S.A."

Composition limbs; flesh-colored paint is flaking off in some places

J.D. KESTNER, GIRL

(LEFT) This doll, with a celluloid shoulder head, kid body, and bisque lower arms, was made by Kestner c.1915. The body is a fine example of the high-quality kid bodies made in Germany at the time. Ht: 18in (46cm)

Light brown mohair wig

Manufacturer's trademark, attached to kid torso

Lead pin joints at elbows and shoulders

Lower arms and tiny hands are made of bisque

The mark is incised on the shoulder head of the doll.

The paper label indicates that the body is stuffed with cork.

Hinged joints at hips and knees

TURTLE-MARK BOY

(LEFT) Made in Germany in the 1930s, this naked boy doll is a typical product of the Rheinische Gummi- und Celluloid-Fabrik. All the facial features are painted. Ht: 10½in (26.5cm)

Molded hair, painted blond

Head and torso molded as one; head does not turn

The raised turtle mark on the back of the head identifies the manufacturer.

Bent arms with molded hands

Body is jointed at hips and shoulders

Legs are molded with dimpled knees

Five molded toes on each foot

Mass-produced Dolls

· 1900s to 1980s ·

FROM THE 1900S TO MID-1950S, millions of celluloid dolls were produced. Some were good quality, such as those manufactured by the Rheinische Gummi- und Celluloid-Fabrik, but many were quite poorly made. Throughout the 1920s and 1930s, celluloid novelty dolls were very popular. Cheap and cheerful, these little trinkets were usually mass-produced in Japan and given away as carnival prizes, or sold at the seashore for a small sum.

By the mid-1950s, doll manufacturers in Germany, the United States, France, and England had stopped using celluloid for dolls, owing to its flammability. Instead, they preferred to work with new and safer plastics, such as vinyl. In some Eastern European countries, such as Poland, celluloid dolls continued to be produced until the late 1980s.

The "K" trademark identifies the doll manufacturer, Kaliskie Zaklady.

Upper eyelashes made of black nylon bristle; lower lashes painted in brown

Dark brown nylon wig, in fashionable style of the day

Hair tied at back of neck with green nylon ribbon

Checked-cotton mini-dress in style of 1960s–1970s

Socket head allows head to turn

Plump upper arms; jointed at shoulders

Molded fingers are slightly webbed; separate thumb

Rounded stomach of a toddler

Bent lower arms with molded hands

Straight legs are sturdy and thick-set

Center seams visible on legs

Small feet with indistinct, molded toes

POLISH DOLL, BEATA *This all-celluloid toddler doll was produced by the Polish manufacturer Kaliskie Zaklady in the 1960s or 1970s — at least a decade after the West had ceased making celluloid dolls. The doll is otherwise composed of modern materials: the sleeping eyes are made of plastic, and the wig is nylon.*

HT: 10½in (27cm)

Fashionable, slip-on PVC shoes

The raised mark on the back of the doll shows Petitcollin's trademark of an eagle's head.

Molded and painted mouth, eyes, and nose

Crudely painted facial features

Bright pink pom-pom hair

Betty Boop look-alike

Black doll with movable limbs

Fine organdy apron trimmed with gold ribbon and white lace

Full, checked-cotton skirt with gold-ribbon trim

NOVELTY DOLLS (ABOVE) *These novelty dolls were made in Japan in the 1920s and 1930s. The figure on the right is a tumbling doll. If it is pushed over, it will bounce back up again. Ht: Largest 2½in (6cm); smallest 2in (4.5cm)*

Lead weight in base makes doll bounce back up

FRENCH COSTUME DOLL (LEFT) *Dressed in French provincial costume, this doll was made in the 1920s by the Petitcollin company of Paris, founded in 1914. The costume is highly ornate, but the doll itself is made of thin, rather brittle celluloid. Ht: 8½in (22cm)*

Molded "earphone" hairstyle; hair painted blond

Inset blue glass eyes; painted brows

Molded and painted ribbed stockings and shoes

"Foreign" usually indicates that a doll was made in Japan.

Molded hair; faint signs of paint remain

Two black dots indicate eyes; no lashes

Molded, closed mouth is crudely painted

Dress made c.1960; the fabric is possibly older

Well-formed hands, with separate fingers and thumbs

Mold cast lines have not been cleaned

JAPANESE PAIR (RIGHT) *Mass-produced in Japan in the 1920s and 1930s, these small figures are low-quality, all-celluloid dolls. The facial features are molded and crudely painted, and much of the dolls' color has now faded. Ht: Largest 5in (12.5cm); smallest 2in (4.5cm)*

GERMAN DOLL (RIGHT) *With its blue eyes, blond hair, and tidy appearance, this doll reflects the 1930s Germanic ideal. The turtle-in-a-diamond trademark indicates that it was made by the Rheinische Gummi- und Celluloid-Fabrik. Ht: 15½in (38.5cm)*

Well-shaped celluloid limbs

Vogue Dolls, Inc.

· 1940s to 1960s ·

JENNIE GRAVES was already established as a designer and producer of fine dolls' clothing when she founded Vogue Dolls, Inc., in 1948. Since the 1930s, she had purchased American- and German-made undressed dolls, clothed them with her own creations, and sold them through stores nationwide; but in 1948, she introduced Ginny, a doll of her own design. ∽ Other dolls were added – each with its own personalized accessories and outfits based on contemporary fashions – to create the Ginny Doll Family. The line included Ginnette (Ginny's baby sister), Jill (her older sister), and Jeff, who could be either Jill's boyfriend or the two sisters' brother. Every doll that was created represented the company's family tradition of producing quality dolls "that are made to be loved."

Light brown corduroy hat, trimmed with blue satin

Brown sleeping eyes, with painted brows and lower lashes

Closed mouth, painted red

Elephant-shaped blue buttons cover the hook-and-eye fastenings

Auburn mohair wig

Upper eyelashes are made of animal hair

Light brown corduroy jacket and skirt, lined with blue satin

Composition head and body, jointed only at neck, shoulders, and hips

Black and gold "Vogue" label stuck on skirt

Skating costume covers a blue satin all-in-one undergarment

Hands are molded into an expressive up-and-outward attitude

Legs are quite straight below the knee, but have shapely thighs

White socks just visible inside skates

Feet are flat and stubby, with no instep

THE SKATER This 1947 doll wears Vogue clothes designed by Jennie Graves, but predates the original Ginny. It has the same all-composition construction as the first Ginnies, which were somewhat shorter, standing only 8in (20cm) tall. The Skater is one of a group that represents various sporting activities: there is also a skier, a golfer, and a tennis player.

Paperlike white cloth skates have metal blades

HT: 14in (35cm)

Synthetic wig, made of Dynel

Head turns from side to side when doll is "walked"

Molded and painted hair

Red painted finger- and toenails

Body is jointed only at shoulders and hips

White flannel dress jacket

Cummerbund around waist matches bow tie

Jill's corsage, trimmed with a pink bow, matches her dress

Trousers embellished with satin tuxedo stripe

Seamed thigh-high stockings

Black and silver glittery socks

Black plastic shoes, fastened with ribbon

Clear plastic open-toe high-heel shoes decorated with sparkles

JILL AND JEFF (LEFT) In his smart evening clothes, Jeff is all set to escort his friend – or sister – Jill to their high-school prom. The dolls are models that were both copyrighted in 1957. They are made of hard vinyl, and have blue sleeping eyes, with molded lashes and painted eyebrows. Ht: Jill 9¾in (24.5cm); Jeff 10in (25cm)

Body made of beige nylon plush fabric

Felt ears

Glass eyes

Printed tartan overcoat, labeled "GINNY'S PUP"

Untinted, molded curls on forehead and around face

Golden brown sleeping eyes, with molded lashes

Wig made of black Dynel

Separate thumb fits into the doll's mouth

GINNY'S PUP (ABOVE) This miniature toy terrier is one of the many accessories made especially for Ginny. Ht: 3½in (9cm)

GINNETTE (RIGHT) Made in the 1960s of tinted soft vinyl, Ginnette has the typical dumpy limbs of a baby doll, and a nursing mouth designed to take a feeding bottle or the doll's thumb. Ht: 8in (20cm)

All-composition Ginny doll model, jointed at shoulders and hips

MISS 2000

Reverse of wrist tag

Ginny Doll Family
FASHION LEADERS IN DOLL SOCIETY

Front of wrist tag reads "Hi! I'm Ginnette/Created by VOGUE DOLLS Incorporated, Malden, Mass."

Dimpled bent limbs

MISS 2000 (LEFT) The "Half-Century Group" was designed between 1948 and 1950. It featured the futuristically clad Miss 2000 and the Misses 1900, 1910, 1920, 1930, 1940, and 1950. A complete set is a real find. Ht: 8in (20cm)

American Manufacturers
· 1900s to the present day ·

A NUMBER OF DOLL MANUFACTURERS were established in the United States throughout the first quarter of the twentieth century, and some of them survive today in one form or another. Most of these manufacturers gained international reputations for their production or design of composition dolls – expertise that they later skillfully adapted to suit the new and exciting potential of plastic.

The Ideal Novelty and Toy Company of Brooklyn, New York, got off to a flying start when founders Morris Michtom and A. Cohn launched their "unbreakable" composition dolls. During the 1930s, Ideal issued a number based on famous film personalities: its Shirley Temple line, in particular, was extremely successful. After World War II, Ideal used its skills to create dolls made of all kinds of plastic; many were best-sellers.

Genuine woven straw hat

Gold-colored plastic "Shirley Temple" brooch

Curly nylon "Shirley Temple" wig

Sleeping plastic eyes, with nylon upper lashes

Reverse socket head

Facial features are modeled on those of Shirley Temple

Smiling open mouth, with teeth

Shoulder joints allow arms to rotate

Slightly bent arms

Printed cotton shirt has corduroy collar and white plastic buttons

Middle fingers of right hand are molded together

Straight legs, with shapely thighs

Joints at hips allow movement of legs

Doll is dressed as fictional character Rebecca of Sunnybrook Farm

Separate fingers on left hand

Body is all-vinyl construction

Blue cotton knee-length trousers

Flat feet allow the doll to stand unaided

Molded toes, with toenail detail

Corduroy cuffs on rolled-up trousers

Knitted cotton knee-length socks

SHIRLEY TEMPLE *The Ideal Novelty and Toy Company first issued Shirley Temple dolls in the 1930s, when little Shirley was the number one box office attraction in the United States. This 1960s hard vinyl version is modeled on the heroine of the film* Rebecca of Sunnybrook Farm, *in which Shirley Temple starred in 1938.*

Black plastic slip-on shoes

HT: 12in (30cm)

Original packaging, with clear plastic film front and Ideal logo

Rooted nylon hair, styled into ringlets

1930S SHIRLEY TEMPLE (RIGHT) One of the original Shirley Temple models, this doll was designed by Bernard Lipfert. Side-glancing eyes and a head of golden "Shirley Temple" curls give it an irresistible appeal. From 1934 to 1938, more than six million dolls of this popular young actress were sold. Ht: 25½in (64cm)

Flirty, sleeping eyes move from side to side and open and close

Composition reverse socket head

Bent composition arms

Cotton shoes conceal straight composition legs

1982 SHIRLEY TEMPLE
(ABOVE) Ideal marketed this updated Shirley Temple in its Classic Doll line. The head is made of soft vinyl, with a hard vinyl body that looks much the same as the 1960s model. The clothing is cotton, with cloth lace-up shoes. Ht: 8½in (22cm)

© IDEAL 1982 HONG KONG

The copyright mark indicates that the doll was made in Hong Kong for Ideal in 1982.

CAMPBELL KID (BELOW) Just one of a range used to advertise Campbell's soups, this composition doll was licensed for production to E.I. Horsman in 1911. Horsman went on to produce a number of character dolls made of plastic. Ht: 12in (30cm)

Painted facial features

Composition arms are jointed at shoulders

Chest label advertises Campbell's Soup

Overalls conceal composition legs, jointed at hips

ANNE SHIRLEY (BELOW) Effanbee (the trademark of Fleischaker and Baum, in New York) drew on L.M. Montgomery's novel Anne of Green Gables to create its all-composition Anne Shirley in 1936. The high quality of Effanbee's composition dolls was maintained in later plastic models. Ht: 15in (38cm)

Human hair wig, a replacement dating from the early 1960s

Sleeping eyes

Composition arms are jointed at shoulders

Flat feet are painted to resemble shoes and socks

Molded hair, with baby curls

Composition flange neck head

Bent composition limbs

Doll wears lacy knit coat over long knitted dress and bootees

1924 GRUMPY (LEFT) This cloth and composition doll from Effanbee was first issued in 1914. Grumpy dolls proved very popular, and many companies included one among their products. Ht: 14½in (36.5cm)

Smock conceals all-composition construction

Cotton smock with heart motif

The Changing Face of Barbie

· 1959 to the present day ·

LEGENDARY "TEEN-AGE FASHION MODEL" BARBIE is probably one of the best known of all modern dolls. Inspired by the risqué Lilli – a mid-1950s cartoon character in the German newspaper *Bild-Zeitung* – Barbie was developed by California-based Mattel, Inc., from one of the original Lilli dolls. The first Barbie was issued in 1959 and represented a stylized adult female. The doll had an elegant, slim waist, high, shapely breasts, and long, slender limbs; her facial features were exaggerated with heavy make-up. The clothing followed the most fashionable styles of the day and seemed to be fantasy – or at least idealized – creations.

Since the 1960s, Barbie's facial features have been greatly modified. Models from the 1980s and 1990s have a natural, youthful appearance, with smiling mouths and wide eyes. Their clothes and accessories are designed to reflect changing lifestyles.

Simulated mother-of-pearl hair decoration

Nylon (saran) hair is rooted into the head

Reverse socket head, made of soft vinyl

Open/closed, slightly thin-lipped mouth is fixed into a broad smile

Wide-staring eyes, painted turquoise and black

Hard vinyl arms are bent at elbows

Shoulder joints allow circular, horizontal, and vertical movement

Plastic "diamond" jewelry

Hard plastic body

Hip-length bodice in stretch nylon

Sumptuous ball gown has layers of vibrant pink-and-silver net over a pink nylon underskirt

Rigid legs, jointed only at hips

Swivel waist enables the torso to turn a full 360°

Feet are molded into standing-on-toes position

Flexible toes

"HAPPY HOLIDAYS" BARBIE

A standard model, made in China, this Special Edition 1990 Barbie comes with a signed photograph. It has numerous outfits and can also wear those of similar-sized dolls.

HT: 12in (30cm)

Arched
eyebrows

Flirtatious, side-
glancing eyes, with
molded eyelashes

Pert mouth

Painted eyes look
straight ahead

Pouting red
lips, drawn
into a slight
smile

DOLL MARKS

The Mattel, Inc., mark and
copyright date are pressed
into the back of the head.

*©MATTEL INC 1966
CHINA*

The body mark appears at
the back of the torso on the
waist or right buttock.

The Barbie logo is
distinctive and has changed
little over the years.

Barbie®

1950s LILLI (ABOVE) The
original Lilli dolls were vampish,
reflecting the exploits of the cartoon
character. This German model is
made of hard vinyl, with a reverse
socket head. Ht: 12in (30cm)

1962 "BUBBLE-CUT BARBIE"
(ABOVE) With her short hairdo —
new in 1962 — "Bubble-cut Barbie"
has all the sophistication, but none
of the toughness, of the Lilli dolls.
Ht: 12in (30cm)

1991 FULL-OF-LIFE BARBIE
(ABOVE) Registered in 1990, this
model glows with youth and vitality.
The doll has a lean body and wears
bright, wash'n'wear clothes from the
"Ski Fun" set. Ht: 12in (30cm)

BARBIE'S FERRARI (RIGHT) This
doll-sized car, made in Italy in
1990 for Mattel, is a scale-model
version of a Pininfarina 328 GTS.
Inside, a 1990 Barbie wears an
outfit from the "Springtime
Fashions" set.

Barbie Ferrari

"Chrome" hubcaps,
with Ferrari
horse logo

Authentic styling details include rearview
wing mirrors and snap-in seat belts

Soft polyethylene
head, with rooted
nylon hair

Outfit is a
perfect replica
of the official
American
Airlines
uniform

Catalog
contains
outfits for
Barbie, boy-
friend Ken,
and best
friend Midge

Original
1950s
Mattel,
Inc., logo

Emergency
phone numbers

**"AMERICAN AIRLINES
STEWARDESS"** (RIGHT) Clothes
transform the basic Barbie into
myriad roles. This set was made
c.1963, and is modeled here
by one of the earliest dolls.
Ht: 12in (30cm)

Regulation
black
shoulder
bag

Barbie baby-sits!
EVERYTHING BARBIE NEEDS TO BABY-SIT
Midge
BABYSITTER

School books with
carrying strap

Miniature regulation
flight bag has a
working zipper

AMERICAN AIRLINES

BABY-SITTER KIT (LEFT) The
"Barbie baby-sits!" set, just one
of Barbie's many accessories,
was introduced in 1962, and
came complete with a pair of
reading glasses, a telephone for
essential calls, and pretzels to munch.

Sandals replace
original classic
high-heel pumps

English Manufacturers

· 1950s to 1980s ·

ENGLISH DOLL-MAKING thrived in the middle years of the twentieth century. A number of firms that had begun production in the 1920s and 1930s coped admirably with the new developments in manufacturing techniques and materials, created their own distinctive style and designs, and were often very successful.

By the mid-1980s, however, financial difficulties had driven many companies out of business altogether. Others had become absorbed by larger international corporations, which moved the manufacturing of their dolls to other countries, especially those in eastern Asia, where labor was cheaper and production costs were lower. The dolls on these pages were made by some of the most prestigious firms of the 1950s to the 1980s.

Printed card in metal ring, attached to the doll's wrist by a string.

Long, rooted nylon hair can be brushed into bangs

Socket head can turn

Stylized facial features

Painted brown eyes, with painted black upper lashes and a tinge of blue eyeshadow above

Hard vinyl body is jointed at shoulders

Torso is made in two parts but does not turn

Molded hands, with joined fingers and separate thumbs

Joints at hips allow movement of legs

Flat feet, with no instep, enable the doll to stand unaided

Doll wears a good-quality cotton gingham dress over white cotton underpants

Wrist tag is the doll's only marking

Straight legs, with rounded calves

Leather shoes, with snap-fastening ankle straps

TRENDON, SASHA DOLL *Sasha Morgenthaler of Zurich, Switzerland, designed the Sasha line of hard vinyl dolls, first produced by Trendon Ltd. of Stockport, Cheshire, UK, in 1965. Girls, boys, and babies were available in three colorings: the flesh tone varied, depending on whether the doll had blond, brunette, or black hair. This example is Sasha Brunette No. 103, issued in 1970.*

HT: 16in (40cm)

Prototype heads are made of plaster, painted in watercolors

Various hair colors are available

Daisy, with the original English-language packaging for a fashion outfit

Side-glancing eyes suggest a youthful girl, full of fun

Final chosen version of the Daisy head

DAISY PROTOTYPES (ABOVE) Mary Quant designed a number of different types of face for Daisy until she was satisfied that the features of the doll represented those of a typical English "model girl."

PEDIGREE, KELLY (RIGHT) Kelly, a fully poseable fashion doll, was designed by Bruce Beresford and produced by Pedigree Soft Toys Ltd. exclusively for a chain of retail stores in the United Kingdom. Kelly was briefly available at the end of 1979. Ht: 11in (28cm)

MARY QUANT'S DAISY (LEFT) The dress designer Mary Quant, working with Flair Toys, introduced Daisy in 1973, and it was produced for ten years. Although Mary Quant designed all of the clothing, much of it was manufactured in Hong Kong, along with the doll itself. Ht: 9in (23cm)

Socket head can turn

Chestnut brown, rooted saran hair

Mary Quant's trademark gives the doll its name

Sleeping blue plastic eyes, with nylon lashes

Painted closed mouth

Dress conceals soft vinyl body

Cotton dress designed by Hazel Smith

Rooted nylon hair

Painted facial features

Reverse socket head is made of soft vinyl

ROSEBUD (RIGHT) Eric and Hazel Smith of Northampton registered the name Rosebud as a trademark for a line of dolls in 1947. This model, manufactured in 1963, has a pretty dolly face. Ht: 18½in (47cm)

Straight legs are jointed at hips

Molded and painted hair

Inset eyes, without lashes

Body is jointed at shoulders

Bent limbs

Joints at hips allow legs to move

White vinyl shoes, with button fastening

All-plastic, injection-molded body

RODDY DOLL (LEFT) Using a combination of their names, doll-makers D.G. Todd and J. Robinson created a line of dolls called Roddy in the late 1930s. This typical injection-molded baby doll was manufactured c.1955. Ht: 12in (30cm)

Buttoned armchair is made of vinyl

Baby and Toddler Dolls

· 1940s to the present day ·

ENCOURAGED BY ADVANCES in equipment and technology in the 1930s, manufacturers of baby dolls began to produce models that were ever more realistic. Those that "performed" in some way – feeding, wetting, or crying – proved to be long-term favorites. In recent years, designers have even created dolls that look as if they have diaper rash, and those that will "eat" solid food. With the aid of batteries, some dolls will laugh, crawl, and even repeat words that are spoken to them.

Many models portray newborn babies, and some are available complete with hospital ID bracelets and navel bindings, as well as birth certificates. Some dolls are anatomically correct, made either as boys or as girls. But these have proved controversial, being considered by some people to carry realism too far.

Manufacturer's trademark is molded into upper back of the torso.

Molded hair

Flange neck head is turned to one side

Soft vinyl construction, jointed at shoulders and hips

Molded Effe logo on back of doll

Bent limbs

Flat feet with spread toes are typical of a newborn baby's

Hands are molded in characteristic baby pose

Navel bandage provides authentic detail

Inset plastic eyes; baby dolls usually have sleeping eyes

Open/closed mouth

Wrist band carries label printed with name, imitating hospital ID bracelet

Slightly "baggy" flesh, with folds, wrinkles, and creases

Realistically styled male genitalia

Hands are molded to show typical baby dimples

BIMBOVERO EFFE *Designed in Italy mainly for the English and American markets, this 1980s baby doll was available either as a girl or as a boy. The whole doll is made of soft vinyl and molded so that the flesh resembles that of a newborn baby, with wrinkles, dimples, and skin folds. The doll has a built-in scent of talcum powder and baby lotion.*

HT: 17½in (45cm)

Cardboard cradle forms part of the doll's packaging

Open mouth, with toothless gums

Rooted blond nylon hair

Name of doll is printed on the side of the cradle

Pert expression changes when doll's torso is squeezed

Dress covers abdomen containing voice box

FIRST LOVE (ABOVE)

A newborn baby girl doll, First Love was marketed in the 1980s by the English Pedigree Doll Company, although it was actually manufactured by Berjusa of Spain. The doll is made of soft vinyl and smells of baby lotion. Ht: 15in (35cm)

Side-glancing painted blue eyes, with painted lashes

MOVING MOUTH BABY

(LEFT and ABOVE) Squeezing the abdomen of this baby doll makes its mouth open and close, and elicits a squeak. Manufactured in Hong Kong and copyrighted by Mattel in the United States in 1966, the doll is made of vinyl, and jointed at the shoulders and hips. Ht: 7in (18cm)

Dress conceals all-composition body, jointed at shoulders and hips

Spotted cotton dress and bonnet, over white petticoat and flannelette diaper

Pink shoes, with lace trim, match the dress and pants

Bent limbs

SUNSHINE BABY (LEFT)

Produced by Vogue Dolls in the 1940s, Sunshine Baby is a true classic of its era. Ht: 8in (20cm)

Vogue Dolls® is a registered trademark of Dakin, Inc. All Vogue Dolls Designs © 1993 Dakin, Inc., Woodland Hills, California, USA, reproduced here courtesy of Dakin.

"POTTY TIME" QUINTS

(BELOW) The "Drink and Wet" set is just one in the Quints line copyrighted in 1991 by Tyco Industries, Inc., of New Jersey and made in China. Each of these tiny toddler dolls has a pair of pants and a baby bottle, and they come with a bench that contains five heart-shaped potties. Ht: 2½in (6cm)

Decorative red ribbons are sewn onto dress and bonnet

Blond hair is tied up in a ponytail with ribbon

Curly rooted saran hair

Reverse socket head

Soft vinyl construction, jointed at shoulders and hips

Open mouth for bottle

Color-coordinated pants match the potty seats

Each of the five potty seats is identified with a color and number

Hole at bottom of torso for liquid to come out

Plastic baby bottles can be filled with water

Royal Doulton and Nisbet

· 1980 to 1985 ·

IN THE FIRST HALF of the 1980s, two English firms joined forces to manufacture several series of collectors' dolls: Royal Doulton, a porcelain company renowned for its figurines and table china; and the House of Nisbet, already well known for its costume dolls. The dolls' porcelain heads and lower arms were created by Eric Griffiths, who had formerly worked for the famous Pedigree Doll Company. Alison Nisbet – daughter of Nisbet's founder, Peggy – designed their stuffed calico bodies and clothing. Most of the series were issued in editions limited to 3,000 or 5,000. Each doll was individually boxed and came with a certificate bearing the limited edition number. Production ceased in 1985.

Real feathers decorate the hat

Soft brown velvet hat

Long curled mohair wig

Well-modeled porcelain shoulder head

Painted facial features

Shoulder head is sewn to body through holes in front and back of shoulder plate

Luxuriant feel and appearance of the fabrics complement the fine quality and modeling of the porcelain head and lower arms

Stuffed calico upper arms and torso, with disk joints at the shoulders

Porcelain lower arms, with hands molded into an expressive gesture

Velvet muff is attached to one wrist

Wrist tag announces the Royal Doulton/ Nisbet partnership, as well as the name of the doll

Stuffed calico legs are stitched to torso at hips

Seams at tops of thighs allow doll to sit

Textured satin dress is trimmed with crushed velvet at neck, wrist, and hem

Crudely shaped feet, with no toes

WINTER *Drawings by the artist Kate Greenaway inspired a series of Collectors' Dolls, issued in 1981, whose elegant period costumes have a seasonal theme. In this example, the doll is dressed in deep, rich red and brown – colors traditionally associated with winter. The lavish velvet trimmings generate a sense of genuine warmth and comfort.*

HT: 10½in (27cm)

THREE-PIECE HEAD MOLD

(*LEFT*) *The plaster mold for the porcelain head is in three parts, held together by thick elastic bands. Bone china slip is poured into the hole at the top and, when it has hardened, the casts are removed. Called "blue heads" because of their color at this stage, they need to be smoothed down before firing.*

Side of shoulder plate　　*Hole for pouring in bone china slip*

DOLL MARKS

Every doll bears the Royal Doulton copyright mark on the shoulder plate.

Special collections have their own individual copyright mark.

MADE IN ROYAL DOULTON ENGLAND
ENGLAND BONE CHINA
D.N.19
© ROYAL DOULTON
TABLEWARE LTD. 1981
KATE GREENAWAY
DOLL COLLECTION

Limited-edition dolls come with a certificate of authentication.

Royal Doulton
NISBET

FACE PAINTING (*RIGHT*) *After the heads are smoothed and fired, they are given either a pink or an ivory matte glaze. Then the facial features are painted and fired several times to set each color. The outline of the eyes and lashes come first, then the irises and pupils. Adding blush pink color to the lips and cheeks gives the finishing touch.*
Head ht: 2½in (6cm)

Collectors' series doll heads are all identical

Eye color changes according to model of doll

Feather duster, made of real feathers

SATURDAY GIRL (*LEFT*)
"Saturday's child works hard for a living," from the children's birthday rhyme, provides the theme for one of the first dolls produced under the Royal Doulton/Nisbet name.
Ht: 10½in (27cm)

Shoulder-length blond mohair wig

Doll wears a maid's uniform

Stuffed calico hands, with the fingers indicated only by stitches; later models have porcelain hands

Cardboard label hanging from wrist identifies the doll and the series to which it belongs

Flange neck head

Painted hair and features

Full, pouting lips give the doll a distinguished mouth

Plastic socket joints at shoulders and hips allow the limbs to move freely

Porcelain lower arms

Porcelain lower legs to above knees

FIRSTBORN (*ABOVE*) *The baby doll of the Royal Doulton/ Nisbet series was issued in 1982. Its dumpy calico body is rather out of keeping with the well-cast porcelain head and lower limbs, but the doll's charm lies in its appearance when clothed. Ht: 12in (30cm)*

~ Men and Boys ~

· 1960s to the present day ·

THE NUMBER OF MALE DOLLS has always tended to be small compared to the number of females, reflecting the industry's belief that boys do not play with dolls. More male models are being produced, as it becomes clear that children of both sexes like to play with dolls of all kinds. ∾ The best-known male doll is G.I. Joe, or Action Man as it was named in the United Kingdom, first issued in 1964. G.I. Joe was inescapably macho, and very much a military man. As antiwar feelings grew in the late 1960s, so G.I. Joe's popularity waned, and the doll was re-marketed in the form of a "global adventurer." Production ceased in the 1980s, but in 1993 Hasbro, the copyright-holder, launched the doll with new and updated accessories.

MADE IN ENGLAND BY PALITOY UNDER LICENCE FROM HASBRO © 1964

Raised, molded mark on torso indicates manufacturer and copyright-holder.

Waterproof suit made of unbleached calico

Molded hair; later models have flock hair

Painted eyes and eyebrows

Molded and painted scar on cheek

Soft vinyl socket head turns a full 360°

Diving belt has metal weights

Torso is fully formed, with well-molded pectoral muscles

Identity tag bears Action Man logo

Jointing at waist allows torso to swivel 360°

Waterproof calico mittens, elasticized at the wrist

Hard vinyl body, with ball and socket joints at hips and waist

Well-modeled hands, showing knuckles and fingernails, are specially designed to grip "equipment"

Hinged ball and socket joints at knees, elbows, shoulders, wrists, and ankles allow them to move freely

Shapely legs have distinctive calf muscles, with visible tendons

Plastic helmet finished to look like brass; air hose attaches to the back

Long, arched feet have well-shaped toes with toenails

Plastic sheath knife is strapped to the calf with elastic

Plastic boots, with metallic weighted clogs

1964 ACTION MAN *Described as "The movable fighting man," the first Action Man has 20 moving parts and can be posed to run, kneel, sit, crawl, stand, or lie flat. When immersed in water, the deep-sea diver set shown here creates surprisingly realistic underwater effects.*

HT: 12in (30cm)

The "Official Action Soldier," dressed in U.S. Army regulation denims

G.I. JOE'S SCOUT CAR
(BELOW) All kinds of toy military vehicles have been produced for G.I. Joe, and models have been updated in keeping with actual changes taking place in the armed forces.

Scout car based on World War II models

Molded and painted hair

Felt cowboy hat

Wrist tag reads "Hi! I'm Jimmy"

Metal toy gun on wrist ribbon

Blue cotton dungarees conceal soft vinyl body, with dimpled limbs

JIMMY (ABOVE) Similar to Ginnette (see page 113), this doll was also made by Vogue Dolls, Inc. Ht: 8in (20cm)
Vogue Dolls® is a registered trademark of Dakin, Inc. Vogue Dolls designs © 1993 Dakin, Inc., Woodland Hills, California, USA, reproduced here courtesy of Dakin.

MATTEL'S 1961 KEN (BELOW)
The advertising slogan "He's a doll" introduced Ken, Barbie's boyfriend (see page 116), in 1961. The first model had a semihard vinyl head and hard vinyl body. The doll's expression and slender physique suggest a clean-living, shy young man. Ht: 12in (30cm)

Luxuriant, rooted nylon hair

Shirt conceals bent arms, with modified ball joints at shoulders

Torso pivots slightly at the waist

Set includes hair gel, booklet with styling tips, and five hair accessories

Molded and painted hair

Painted green eyes

Movable head

Blond flock "crew-cut" hair

Painted eyes, with molded lids and lashes

Suit conceals straight, unjointed arms and legs

Small hands, with indented fingernails

Simple packaging, printed in one language

Sophisticated packaging, printed in several languages

Doll's name is printed on T-shirt

Hard vinyl limbs, tinted to give the doll a suntanned appearance

1991 "ULTRA HAIR" KEN
(ABOVE) As with Barbie, Mattel has made major alterations to Ken, to keep pace with changing trends. This model has the well-muscled body of an athletic young man, and hair that can be coiffed with styling gel. Ht: 12in (30cm)

1991 "COOL SHADES" PAUL
(RIGHT) A boyfriend for Sindy (see page 120), Paul was first issued by Pedigree in the 1960s, withdrawn in 1971, then reissued in 1987. This version is dressed for the beach and wears imitation RayBan sunglasses. Ht: 12in (30cm)

New Doll Ideas

· 1960s to the present day ·

THE BOOM YEARS of the twentieth century saw a change of pace in the doll world. Although the traditional models were as popular as ever, novelty dolls came and went as styles changed. Some reflected the political atmosphere of the time, such as the movement against nuclear weapons, the anarchy of punk rock — or the renewed emphasis on the importance of the family unit. The versatility of plastic, combined with the ingenuity of the manufacturers, allowed ever more complex designs.

〜 Not all modern dolls are plastic. Michael and Lynne Roche of Bath, England, are among a number of individual makers who have returned to using mainly natural materials for their dolls. Beth, one of their designs, shows the best of English doll-making in the 1990s.

Red-blond mohair wig

Well-shaped bisque socket head

Painted mouth

Inset blue glass eyes

Traditionally shaped wooden body

Ball joints at the elbows, shoulders, and wrists

Bisque hands are large and expressive

Ball joints at hips allow doll to sit

Calves are smooth and well carved

Ball joints at knees allow flexibility

Flat feet are carved to show toes

Signature of Michael Roche, maker of the body, inscribed on the right buttock.

The maker's mark appears beneath the hairline on the back of the head.

Initials of Lynne Roche and date of manufacture appear below left ear.

Yellow knitted cardigan has colored wooden buttons

Cat-shaped toy, made of printed cotton, fits snugly into back pocket of doll's dungarees

Blue denim dungarees are fastened at front with wooden buttons

Red leather shoes, with button fastening

HT: 11in (28cm)

BISQUE AND WOODEN DOLL, BETH *Created by Michael and Lynne Roche in Bath, England, in 1992, Beth embodies the 1990s revival of interest in traditional crafts and the use of natural materials. The doll has a turned wooden body and finely cast bisque head and hands. Its clothing is also made from natural fibers: wool and cotton, with leather for the shoes.*

JUDITH "MOTHER AND BABY" (RIGHT) This innovative – if unrealistic – "pregnant" doll, issued in 1992, was designed by Villy Nielsen A/S in Denmark and manufactured by the Lucky Bell Plastics Company in Hong Kong. Ht: 11in (28cm)

1985 PUNK ROCKER
(LEFT) A representative of the punk scene that began in the mid-1970s, this hard vinyl doll is one of a pair issued by Marian Kenny Designs in England. Ht: 7½in (19cm)

FATHER
Ht: 12in (30cm)

Soft vinyl head, with molded hair and painted features

Shirt conceals hard vinyl body, jointed at shoulders and hips

Clothes for boy twin coordinate with those for father

Soft vinyl head

Large, rounded tummy lifts off to allow baby to be removed. Then spring-loaded flat tummy moves into place

Loose-fitting cotton and polyester clothing conceals hard vinyl body

Molded sandals, with painted details

C.N.D. MARCHERS (ABOVE)
The rise of the peace movement in the 1950s and 1960s inspired the design of these two supporters of the British Campaign for Nuclear Disarmament. Manufactured in hard vinyl, the dolls are dressed in beatnik style and wear C.N.D. medallions. Ht: 7½in (19cm)

MOTHER
Ht: 12in (30cm)

Maternity clothes, as well as accessories for the baby, are available

BOY TWIN
Ht: 4in (10cm)

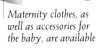

THE HEART FAMILY (BELOW) Mattel, in the United States, created its own nuclear family in 1985, when it packaged two adult dolls together with twin baby dolls. In the six years the Hearts were in production, the line grew to include grandparents, baby cousins, and neighborhood kids.

Vinyl accessories include highchair, baby bath, and pony rocker

Hard vinyl baby doll, with bent limbs

GIRL TWIN
Ht: 4in (10cm)

Mother's outfit matches that of little girl

National Dolls

National dolls take many forms, ranging from folk-art dolls crafted by indigenous peoples to record their culture, and patriotic dolls that celebrate popular heroes or historic events, to souvenir dolls in national costumes, which are not always made in the country they are intended to represent. In some cases the designs or materials used have changed over the years, but many national dolls are still made in accordance with centuries-old traditions.

THE NOTION OF NATIONAL DOLLS developed in the eighteenth century, as many more Europeans ventured abroad. People collected dolls as mementos of their travels. In some countries, no tradition of national dolls existed. Europeans introduced the concept, with the aim of recording the different ways of life and costumes in these places – sometimes with commercial advantages for the Europeans themselves.

Dolls in China and Japan

The best known of the national dolls are the Japanese festival dolls. For more than 400 years, these figures have been used for very specific purposes. Boys are taught the virtues of manliness, loyalty, and chivalry; and girls are trained to understand the duties and virtues of being a good wife and mother. The children also learn of their nation's history and culture through this process. These dolls are put on display only once a year, on the appropriate festival day – March 3 for girls, and May 5 for boys (see pages 132–133).

⁓ At *Tango no sekku*, the Boys' Festival, the doll display is set out on a two- or three-tiered stand.

Dolls representing samurai warriors and legendary characters are featured, as well as miniature models of swords, banners, hats, and horses. *Ohina matsuri*, the Girls' Festival, is more complex. As a mother and daughter set out the dolls on a five- or seven-tiered stand, the mother explains the significance of each of the figures. Models of the Emperor and Empress, court officials, and musicians and servants are included among the dolls. Miniature household furnishings are also shown, and are placed on the lower tiers. Various personal objects that represent the dowry of a bride from a noble or samurai family, and offerings of rice cakes and sake, are also displayed on the lower tiers.

⁓ Over the years, the dolls have changed hardly at all. The makers stay faithful to the traditional styles with as much accuracy as is possible, and do not try to develop or improve on the designs.

⁓ *Kokeshi* are another, entirely different, kind of traditional Japanese doll.

SOUTH AFRICAN MISSION DOLL (*LEFT*) *This stuffed felt doll and its intricately beaded costume were made in a Red Cross Rehabilitation Center in Durban, c.1960. Dolls like this were sold to raise money in support of the center. Ht: 13in (33cm)*

MEXICAN PAPIER-MACHE DANCER (*RIGHT*) *A traditional design of brightly painted papier-mâché was the inspiration for this Mexican doll, which was made in 1991. It is a folk-art doll and is rather crude, but colorful. The doll's arms and legs are jointed with elastic. Ht: 13in (33cm)*

KOKESHI CRAFTSMAN IN JAPAN (LEFT) *Each maker of the turned wooden* kokeshi *may give his dolls a slightly different shape and paint them in his own special signature design. Whole "families" of these traditional* kokeshi *are made, in a wide range of sizes.*

NEW ORLEANS SUGAR-CANE CUTTER (RIGHT) *This wax figure is one of a series of dolls that portray the traditional trades of the state of Louisiana. It was made by a member of the Vargas family, sometime between 1915 and the 1930s. Ht: 7in (18cm)*

They have been made in the northeastern region of Japan since the early seventeenth century. *Kokeshi* are fashioned from turned wood and given a decorative painted finish. These dolls are limbless, having only a head and a body. Originally designed as religious symbols, *kokeshi* became toys for children; nowadays they are sold mainly as souvenirs.

∽ In China, children played not with dolls, but with small, brightly colored clay figures, often representing animals. Dolls in the Western style were introduced by

Europeans to help to preserve a record of the way of life in China. Many dolls such as these were made at missions that had been set up toward the end of the nineteenth century to aid children in need. Found mainly in the southern provinces of Kiangsu, Fukien, and Chekiang, carved wooden dolls, such as those from the Door of Hope Missions (see pages 134–135), were dressed by the children and sold to raise funds for the missions themselves. Dolls were also sold as souvenirs in the markets and bazaars of China. These were made out of wire and clay, or painted plaster, and represented theatrical dancers and performers.

Dolls of Russia

The *matryoshka*, or nesting dolls, have long been associated with Russia (see pages 136–137), although the idea for dolls that fit inside each other probably comes from China. Various styles of doll were traditionally made in Russia, as in other eastern European countries, to record the peoples, costumes, and culture of the different regions; today they are produced primarily as souvenirs to sell to tourists. Customarily, wood was used to make these dolls, but in recent years, rag has often been used.

∽ National dolls, especially the folk-art kind, are always popular with foreign visitors, but they have a value far greater than mere souvenirs. They provide paid employment for the makers, help to record the customs and traditions of the country, and preserve the craft of doll-making itself.

BRAZILIAN RAG COUPLE (RIGHT) *These are fairly sophisticated Brazilian rag dolls, made in the 1930s, with embroidered bodies and facial features and anatomical detail. Their costumes are cleverly worked; the woman's has additional decoration in the form of colored pieces of tinfoil. In both cases, the fingernails are shaped using small pieces of opaque celluloid. Ht: 18in (46cm)*

Japanese Dolls

· 1900s to 1960s ·

MANY JAPANESE DOLLS are designed not as playthings but as ornaments, often depicting some aspect of Japanese history or culture. The intriguing *sakura-ningyō* (cherry dolls) may be modeled on Kabuki dancers, or they may portray some aspect of everyday life. It has long been a favorite pastime among young women to make and dress these figures. Today, cherry dolls are also produced commercially, mainly for export or as souvenirs, but they are still popular display items in Japanese homes. ⁓ Dolls in the decorative category known as *hiña-ningyo* (festival dolls) serve a second purpose. Brought out only on the children's festival days each year, these dolls, which are handed down from generation to generation, are used to illustrate the traditions of the nation.

Gilt metal comb adorns the hair

Gofun-covered socket head

Floor-length wig made from human hair

Inset glass eyes, with painted eyebrows

Mouth is outlined, with finely painted detail on lips

Wooden fan, with painted decoration

Green silk kimono over white damask kimono

Cloth upper arms and thighs

Composition lower limbs and torso, painted to match coloring of the head

Stylized hands with long fingers

Well-shaped torso has rounded belly and molded breasts

Feet are flat and molded to show toes

Long silk crepe trousers

HT: 13in (33cm)

CEREMONIAL FIGURE WITH FAN *Representing the wife of a high-ranking official of the court, this majestic figure in ceremonial robes dates from the early 20th century. The doll has an unusually extensive wardrobe of elaborate costumes, which are made of silk and damask.*

Plaster composition head and hands

MOUNTED WARRIOR
(LEFT) An important element of Tango-no-sekku, the Boys' Festival, this ornate figure is part of the set that conveys the code of the samurai, Japan's aristocratic warrior class. Ht: 10in (25cm)

SHOKI, THE DEVIL CHASER
(RIGHT) By tradition, Japanese families displayed an image of a legendary character, Shoki, at the Boys' Festival in the belief that he would protect their sons from evil. This figure is a late 19th-century doll, designed to hold only one pose. Ht: 22in (55cm)

Horse is made of a padded wire armature covered with animal skin

Padded costume is part of construction of doll and cannot be removed

Silk brocade costume, with gold-painted paper armor

Elaborate robes made of padded silk brocade

Ornaments are carved from wood, then gilded

Carved and lacquered wooden stand

CEREMONIAL PAIR (BELOW)
The figure on the left of this boxed set is described in detail opposite. The other doll represents a man, ready to be dressed as a top-level official of the emperor's court.

Gofun-covered lower limbs and torso

Stand is made of lacquered and painted wood

Gilded wooden feet

Man's face is natural color; high-ranking lady's face is white

Patterned silk kimono, with long sleeves

Hair is a silk wig

Face mask is made of painted, stiffened fabric

Bottom layer of three-tiered black lacquered presentation box; other layers hold clothes and accessories (see page 149)

Feet bear toed socks

SILENT ENVOY (ABOVE) Yamato-ningy○, dolls representing children in traditional dress, were originally designed as gifts for royalty to present to honored guests. More recently, such dolls have been sent as "envoys of friendship" to other countries. Ht: 13in (33cm)

Male figure dressed in silk undergarment; ceremonial robes are included in the set

MAIDEN WITH HATS (RIGHT)
This sakura-ningy○, or cherry doll, portrays a Kabuki character performing the "Dance of the Seven Hats," an interpretation of a Japanese folktale. The doll is commercially made and dates from the 1950s. Ht: 14in (35cm)

Fixed-pose body, made of padded cloth over a wire armature

Hats are made of silk over buckram, trimmed with gold

Doll is mounted on a varnished wooden stand

Chinese Dolls

· 1900s to 1950s ·

FROM THE EARLY NINETEENTH CENTURY to about 1950, almost all dolls and toys in mainland China were made in missions set up to help destitute children – often slaves, child widows, or prostitutes. Europeans were the driving force behind the missions and were hoping to retain the culture of the country while making attractive souvenirs that could be sold to raise funds for the missions' work.

Two important missions were based in Shanghai and Canton under the name Door of Hope. At the Shanghai center, which was opened in 1901, the girls were taught needlework, a skill they could use to dress wooden dolls, for which they were paid. The Canton mission made similar dolls using composition.

Painted eyes and hair

Heads are carved from pear or boxwood and polished smooth

Bright colors and decorative embroidery indicate child is of a higher social class than plainly uniformed nurse

Back of head is carved into a bun shape

Baby is 5½in (14cm) tall

Pink silk "sling" ties the baby to the nurse's back

Child's legs are made of stuffed cloth

Hands are carved from wood and then polished

Traditional suit of tunic over three-quarter-length trousers

Trousers conceal carved wooden legs

Front of costume has faded from exposure to sunlight

Fingers are fashioned together, but thumbs are separate

Clothing is made from scraps of fabric, donated by well-wishers

AMAH AND BABY *Made at one of the Door of Hope missions between 1928 and 1930, these two dolls depict an amah – a child's nurse – carrying a baby on her back. In keeping with the custom for the working class at the time, the nurse's feet are not bound, although those of the baby's mother would be, since she is of a higher social status.*

HT: 10½in (27cm)

Shoes are black silk, with rolled tops and white soles

MISSION DOLL FAMILY (BELOW)
This family of dolls from the 1930s is made of cotton and has embroidered features. The dolls' fingers are formed from loops of cotton. Ht: Largest 3in (7.5cm); smallest 2in (5cm)

The name SHAOHSING INDUSTRIAL MISSION, SHAOHSING, CHEKIANG PROVINCE, CHINA is printed at the top of the card

Molded and painted facial features

Female doll holds composition and cloth baby

Composition head and limbs; body is made of padded cloth over wire armature

Waistband has foil and paper decoration

Long silk dress, with three-quarter-length kimono

Silk costume is richly embroidered

FARMER AND WIFE (BELOW)
These dolls, dressed in the dark blue associated with the post-war revolutionary period, are part of a set designed in the 1950s by Ada Lum. Their purpose was not only to provide a record of rural Chinese costumes, but also to give work to refugees who had fled to Hong Kong from mainland China in the wake of the revolution. Ht: 18in (46cm)

PEKING OPERA CHARACTERS
(ABOVE) Two figures from a set made c.1900, these rare display dolls represent dancers of the Peking Opera. The man's high status is denoted by the elaborate embroidery on his silk costume. Ht: Woman 11in (28cm); man 11½in (29cm)

MANDARIN WITH LONG FINGERS (RIGHT)
Known to have been bought in Hong Kong c.1930, this doll may be one of those from the Door of Hope Mission at Canton. Similar dolls were adapted for use as puppets by attaching bamboo rods to their wrists. Ht: 10in (25cm)

Woolen hair is braided into pigtail

Stuffed cotton head and body

Embroidered eyebrows and eyes

Lips are painted

Ornamental headdress is made of stiffened, painted paper

Head and limbs made of painted composition over wood

Long fingers traditionally indicate that doll represents the aristocracy

Dolls are dressed in matching everyday outfits

Silk brocade costume, heavily ornamented and embroidered

Female has embroidered shoes of a type worn only indoors

Beach grass shoes for outdoor wear

Multiple Heads and Faces

· 1860s to 1980s ·

FROM THE 1860S ONWARD, a number of patents were taken out for dolls with two or three different faces molded on the same head. Fritz Bartenstein and Carl Bergner, both of Germany, were among the major manufacturers of these in the nineteenth century, and Herr Bergner's firm continued until the 1930s. Although a doll with a range of facial expressions does allow play to be more realistic, the doll can look quite hideous because of the head cover that must extend from the shoulder plate to hide the "reserve" faces. The principle of changing faces is still used today, for example, in rag storybook dolls, which show the faces of different characters as the cloth pages are lifted.

⌐ Another similar, if less bizarre, novelty is the doll that has one body and a set of three or four different heads, which may represent a boy and a girl, each with a happy and a sad expression. Such a doll may also have interchangeable limbs, one set being made in a different flesh tone.

HT: 16in (40cm)

TWO-FACED DOLL *Probably made by Fritz Bartenstein in Germany in the 1880s, this doll has an egg-shaped head, molded with two faces and two sets of ears. The detail in the screaming face is pleasingly authentic: apart from the open mouth, the flesh tone is darker than that of the smiling doll, the eyebrows are knitted together into a frown, and the nostrils are red.*

Head is turned by a metal and wooden peg

Fabric-covered carton cap, molded as an extension of the composition shoulder plate

Mohair wig is attached to the head cover

Composition swivel head coated in wax

Painted facial features; eyes are inset blown glass

Two-tiered cape, made of nun's veiling edged with crocheted cotton lace, with satin ribbon tie

Cotton robe, with broderie anglaise bodice and flounces

Doll says "Mama" when voice box within torso is activated by pulling a cord at waist

Hands are painted composition; rest of limbs are made of wood and stuffed pink calico

THREE-FACED BISQUE DOLL

(*RIGHT*) *A cumbersome head cover makes this doll seem particularly unrealistic. A ring at the crown of the wig turns the faces, and a string at waist level operates a speaking mechanism. The doll, which has a composition and calico body and wooden limbs, may have been made by Simon and Halbig for Carl Bergner* c.1890s. *Ht: 12in (30cm)*

Bisque socket head

Mohair wig on thin cardboard head cover conceals two faces

Inset blue glass eyes

Happy face, with smiling mouth

Screaming face, with frown and teardrop

Sleeping face has no eyes, only permanently closed eyelids

Crying face, with furrowed brow and open mouth

Happy face, with "laughing" eyes

THREE-FACED PIXIE (*LEFT*)

A 1960s ceramic baby doll, manufactured in the United States, this may have been based on a model made in celluloid in the 1930s. The doll has no head cover: the hood of the clothing is designed to conceal the extra faces and the turning mechanism. Ht: 16½in (42cm)

THREE-IN-ONE (*BELOW*)

This multiheaded, multilimbed model was made in 1916 by the Doll Pottery Company, one of the few companies set up in England in World War I to produce ceramic doll parts. The set includes parts for a dark-skinned boy and a pale-skinned girl. Head ht: 3½in (9cm)

Molded and painted facial features

Sleeping face has closed eyelids

Molded and painted hair and facial features

Ceramic hands and head

Stoneware shoulder head

Pixie suit covers stuffed cloth body

Head is sewn or pinned to stuffed cloth torso through holes in the shoulder plate

Cloth upper limbs

Two faces portray sad Cinderella and Wicked Stepmother; others show Fairy Godmother, Prince Charming, and Cinderella in a ball gown

STORYBOOK DOLL (*LEFT*)

This 1980s stuffed cotton figure, which tells the traditional tale of Cinderella, is a multiheaded doll of a different kind. Each of the multiple skirts lifts up to reveal the face of a new character, with the text of the story printed below it. Ht: 9in (23cm)

The text features the character shown

CINDERELLA

WICKED STEPMOTHER

Stoneware lower limbs are fastened with string or thread to fabric upper limbs around flange at top

Peddler Dolls

· 1820s to 1990s ·

AS A CONVERSATION PIECE in fashionable drawing rooms in nineteenth-century England, few objects could rival the fascinating peddler doll. Given a prominent place on a whatnot or the mantelpiece, and usually sitting beneath a glass dome to protect it from dust, the peddler doll would be dressed in the traditional red-cloaked costume, carrying a tray or basket overflowing with miniature wares. Most popular between 1820 and 1860, peddler dolls are enjoying a revival today.

Although itinerant traders traveled all over Europe, peddler dolls were a peculiarly English phenomenon. Even so, most were made in Germany and dressed in England. The heads are often wood or composition, but kid, apples, and wax were also used. The bodies are often made of wood, composition, or stuffed cloth.

The maker's mark is stamped in ink on the back of the torso.

Molded and painted facial features

Costume is typical of 19th-century female peddler

Bonnet is molded with the head and hair

Cap frill is made of lace dipped in slip, then fired with the head

Bisque shoulder head attached to the body by strips of sticky-backed fabric

Stuffed calico upper arms and torso, disk joints at shoulders

Bisque lower arms, cast to above wrists

Hands are large and gnarled, like those of an old woman

Stuffed calico upper legs, stitched to torso at hips

Bisque lower legs, with molded and painted stockings and shoes

Basket contents include bead necklaces, books, toys, and miniature dolls

MARTHA THOMPSON DOLL *Some peddler dolls came with an empty basket, to be filled at home with a variety of tiny items, ranging from notions to kitchenware. This peddler was made in the United States by Martha Thompson in the late 1950s, and dressed and equipped by English doll collector Faith Eaton in 1992.*

HT: 12in (30cm)

APPLE-HEAD PEDDLER (RIGHT)
A pickled apple forms the head of this unusual peddler, which was made in England c. 1830. The apple is carved and painted to re-create the wrinkled, weather-beaten features of an old street vendor. Ht: 6in (15cm)

Glass bead eyes set into pickled apple head

Open mouth showing teeth

PEG WOODEN PEDDLER (LEFT)
Made originally as a peg wooden, (see pages 18–19), this peddler dates from about 1900. It was adapted in the 1960s by Hilda Fonteyn, a doll enthusiast living in northern England. Ht: 13in (33cm)

Gray mohair wig, glued on head

Spectacles made of copper wire

Simple painted facial features

Wooden head and torso, with peg-jointed limbs

Equipped with a wide range of knickknacks and miniature household utensils

Colorful clothing hides a crudely made cloth body

Doll is mounted on a varnished wooden stand

Inset silk hair

Painted facial features

Wax shoulder head, molded with bosom and arms

"HENRIETTA" (RIGHT)
Most peddler dolls represent old women, so this example of a young lady is particularly striking. The graceful wax-headed figure, with beautifully formed hands, was made c. 1860 by English wax modeler Henrietta Wade. Ht: 10in (25cm)

Original contents of basket can help to date the doll

Painted hair and facial features

Carved wooden head and torso, with peg-jointed limbs

Padded cloth legs and torso over wire armature

Wooden mount is normally covered by glass dome, which sits in the groove

NOTION NANNY
(RIGHT) Made in the United States c. 1960s, this doll is said to represent a typical peddler of the Ozark mountain range, wandering through parts of Oklahoma, Arkansas, and Missouri. Notion Nanny is one of the names given to peddler dolls in the United States. Ht: 10½in (27cm)

Woven basket holds doll-size metal utensils

Soles of feet are painted to resemble shoes

A Master Doll-maker

· 1970s to the present day ·

TRAINED AS A COSTUME DESIGNER at Parsons School of Design in New York, E.J. Taylor began making dolls in 1973. The first models he created were clowns based on characters from Italy's commedia dell'arte theater. The following year he designed a group of half-man and half-animal figures. Then, in 1976, Taylor created a figure, which he called Lady in White, for Tiffany's jewelry store in New York, and this proved so successful that, two years later, Saks Fifth Avenue asked the artist to produce three more "garden ladies."

Taylor's dolls all have an extraordinary quality: their heads and hands are modeled from Sculpey, a craft clay material developed in the United States that can be fired to a ceramic-like hardness at household oven temperatures; the bodies are made of papier-mâché molded over a wire armature.

Half-closed eyes with heavy eyelids, accentuated with peach coloring

Well-shaped hands with long, elegant fingers, modeled in Sculpey

Straw bonnet is tinted to match the delicate tones of the painted facial features

Traditional Sussex trug contains dried roses

Facial features, modeled from Sculpey clay, have a lifelike quality

Closed, full-lipped mouth is drawn back and indented at the corners

High, spare cheekbones; slackened jaw shows "bone" structure beneath

Clothes conceal body made of papier-mâché molded over a wire armature

Damask silk costume made from a fringed shawl, trimmed with bead buttons

LADY IN WHITE *The first of a group of four "garden ladies," the Lady in White was designed and made by E.J. Taylor in 1976, as a display piece for Tiffany's jewelry store in New York City. The figure portrays an elderly, aristocratic-looking woman dressed in a costume reminiscent of those worn in the early decades of the 20th century.*

HT: 30in (77cm)

Facial features are modeled and painted; human hair wig

Sculpey shoulder head

Branching twigs form the antlers of the reindeer

Elf's outfit is made from scraps of fur, fabric, and leather

Sculpey hands encased in crocheted mittens

Huge flat feet and sticklike legs

Papier-mâché body – Sculpey is too heavy to be used for whole doll

Wire armature provides the skeleton of the doll

Painted hair and facial features

Finely modeled head captures the strong features of a young girl of African origin

Papier-mâché legs, wearing stockings

DOLL IN THE MAKING

(RIGHT) The construction of this figure is typical of Taylor's work. The head, hands, and feet are modeled from Sculpey clay, while the rest of the body and legs are made of papier-mâché over a wire armature. Ht: 27½in (70cm)

Sculpey feet, with shaped instep and heel, allow the doll to stand unaided

JESSIE (ABOVE) This fine head

was created in 1988, using Sculpey III – a clay that has all the features of Super Sculpey, with the bonus of being available in 30 colors. The finished texture of the clay gives the illusion that the figure is made of wax. Head ht: 4in (10cm)

ELF (ABOVE) Created as part

of a Christmas window display commissioned by Tiffany's, New York, in 1981, the elf is riding a stuffed stockinette "hobby horse" reindeer with twig antlers, which is also the work of Taylor. The elf's head is made of Super Sculpey, a type of flesh-tone craft clay with a ceramic-like finish. Ht: 11in (28cm)

MAN
Ht: 13in
(33cm)

Clothing made from scraps of net, lace, silk, burlap, and other fabrics

GROUP OF THREE (LEFT).

Produced in 1981 for Tiffany's Christmas window display, this trio represents three ages of mankind. Taylor also designed and made the clothing for the dolls. The male figure, including the hair, is finished in varying shades of one color, while the two women are dressed in neutral tones, with added vibrance in the old lady's bonnet and the young woman's stomacher.

OLD
WOMAN
Ht: 13in
(33cm)

Expressive hands are a feature of E.J. Taylor dolls

Cotton jacket knitted by E.J. Taylor

YOUNG
WOMAN
Ht: 12in
(30cm)

Crocheted cotton slippers

GEBRÜDER HEUBACH GIRL
*Best known for its character babies,
the German company of Gebrüder
Heubach also created many other
lines, including this* c.1920s *girl
with dolly face. Ht: 16in (40cm)*

QUEEN ELIZABETH II *This bisque shoulder head was modeled in 1970 by Martha Thompson, a doll artist in the United States. The doll's lower arms and legs are also made of bisque, attached to a stuffed calico body. Doll ht: 14in (35cm)*

ORIENTAL GIRL *The bisque socket head of this late 19th-century German doll bears the mark of Schoenau and Hoffmeister. Ht: 14in (35cm)*

∽ Acknowledgments ∽

AUTHOR'S ACKNOWLEDGMENTS

My very grateful thanks to the Wenham Historical Association and Museum, Worthing Museum & Art Gallery, Christie's South Kensington, and Bethnal Green Museum of Childhood for their valuable assistance and cooperation; also Diane Buck, Sally White, Olivia Bristol, Christine Jeffery, Noreen Marshall, Betty Ridley, William Birnbaum, and Josephine Goodfellow. I especially thank Faith Eaton, for allowing the use of her wonderful dolls and for commenting on the text. Likewise, Dorothy and Evelyn Jane Coleman, my American family, deserve special thanks for sharing their vital knowledge as well as their beautiful dolls. I am indebted to everyone at Dorling Kindersley for all their help, in particular Gillian Roberts, my good-humored editor, and Kevin Ryan, who has designed a magnificent book. Many thanks also to Matthew Ward in England and Lynton Gardiner in the United States for their inspired photographs. Finally, to Tiber and Miss Polly, thank you for being so patient.

PUBLISHER'S ACKNOWLEDGMENTS

Dorling Kindersley acknowledges the generous help of those individuals without whom this book could not have been produced. Special thanks to Catherine Sidwell at Bethnal Green Museum of Childhood; Katherine Higgins at Christie's South Kensington; and Linda Stiles and Sally White at Worthing Museum & Art Gallery. Polly Boyd and Lesley Riley worked diligently and with great patience to complete the text pages, supported by Constance Novis; Alex Corrin compiled the index; Charlotte Davies, Alison Edmonds, Chris Legee, and Alison Shackleton provided the team with creature comforts; Sharon Moore helped prepare pages for final film; Julia Pashley researched the archive picture material; Mel Roberts explained the ins and outs of the English language; Ann Thompson gave design assistance; Alastair Wardle contributed his computer expertise.

PUBLIC AND PRIVATE DOLL COLLECTIONS

In the following acknowledgments, abbreviations with page numbers indicate position on page:

t=top; b=bottom; c=center; l=left; r=right

All the dolls photographed for this book belong to the private collection of **Faith Eaton**, except: **Bethnal Green Museum of Childhood** *A branch of the Victoria & Albert Museum* 2, 7 (r), 12 (l, r), 13 (tl, bl, br), 16, 17 (3 dolls bl), 30 (l), 33 (tl, cr), 36, 37, 38, 39 (except bl, br), 40, 41, 57 (2 dolls tr), 60, 65 (bl), 70 (l, r), 71 (br), 79 (br), 84, 85 (tr), 96, 107 (bl), 115 (br), 119 (except tc), 124, 125, 129 (b), 131 (b), 136,139 (2 dolls tl), 143 (br). **Christie's South Kensington** 61 (tl, tr, bl), 101 (br), 148 (br), 149 (tr), 150 (br). **Coleman Collection** 3, 42 (br), 43 (bl), 44, 45 (except tl), 46, 47 (except br), 48, 49 (tl, bl, bc), 50, 51 (tr, tc, c, br), 93 (tr), 97, 99 (tr), 101 (tl, tr). **Courtesy of the Wenham Museum, Wenham, MA.** 1, 6 (br), 9 (tl), 14, 15 (tl, bl), 17 (br), 22, 23 (c, br), 26, 27 (tl, tc, b), 32, 74 (r), 75, 88, 90, 91 (tl, bl, br), 92 (bc), 93 (5 dolls b), 104 (br), 105 (br), 106, 107 (tr, r), 111 (tl, tc), 112, 113 (tl, tc, bl, br), 122 (cl), 127 (tr), 138, 139 (br), 156, 157 (tl). **Worthing Museum & Art Gallery** 3, 11 (tr), 15 (br), 21 (bl, br), 33 (bl), 35(tr, br), 53 (tr), 54 (bl), 55 (bl, tl), 56, 57 (tl, bl), 59 (tl, tc, bl, br), 61 (cr), 62, 63, 65 (br), 69 (tc, bl), 71 (tr), 81 (bl), 87 (br), 128, 139 (tr), 142, 145 (tr), 154. **Other individuals** who kindly lent us either their own dolls or doll-associated items: Chris Dawson 126 (tl); Lucinda and Emma Ganderton 17 (tr), 89 (tl), 121 (br); Hilary Kennelly 120 (tl); exhibit on loan to Worthing

Museum by a former Worthing resident 59 (tl, tc); Carol Wagner Merriman 113 (c); Lynne and Michael Roche 81 (cl), 128; Gunilla Rosengren 101 (bl); Kevin Ryan 9 (bl), 137 (b); E.J. Taylor 30 (br), 146, 147; Matthew Ward 126.

The author and publisher also thank the **following manufacturers** for permission to reproduce their dolls in this book: A.C. Fincken, *Sunny Jim* 95 (tl); Alexander Doll Co., *Dionne Quintuplet Baby* and *Toddler Dolls, Dr. Allan Roy Dafoe* and *Nurse Louise de Kirilene* 26–27; Chad Valley Toys – exclusive to Woolworths', *Dwarfs* from Walt Disney's film *Snow White and the Seven Dwarfs* 99 (b); Dakin, Inc., *Vogue Dolls Girl Scout* 9 (tl), *Waac-ette* and *Wave-ette* 111 (t), *Skater* 112, *Jill* and *Jeff, Ginny's Pup, Miss 2000, Ginnette* all 113, *Sunshine Baby* 123 (lc), *Jimmy Cowboy* 127 (tr), *Davy Crockett* 156. Vogue Dolls® is a registered trademark of Dakin, Inc. All Vogue Dolls designs © 1993 Dakin, Inc., Woodland Hills, California, USA, reproduced by courtesy of Dakin; DC Comics, SUPERMAN, BATMAN and ROBIN™ and © 1993 DC Comics. All rights reserved. Used by permission of DC Comics, 111; Johnny Gruelle's *Raggedy Ann*, copyright © Johnny B. Gruelle, Playskool/Hasbro, Inc., exclusive manufacturer 89; Hasbro International Inc., *Sindy* 120, 121 (tl, tr, bl), *Patch* 121 (c, br), *Action Man* (G.I. Joe, US) 126, 127 (tl); Ideal UK, 1960s *Shirley Temple* 114, 1982 *Shirley Temple* 115 (tl), 1930s *Shirley Temple* 115 (tr); Jesco, *Bisque Kewpie* 86, *Celluloid Kewpies* 104 (br). "The KEWPIE® Trademark and KEWPIE® characters are protected by U.S. Trademark and Copyright Registrations, exclusively licensed to Jesco and reprinted under permission from Jesco." Mattel UK Ltd., *Barbie* 116, 117, *Ken* 127 (bl, bc), *Heart Family* 128 (b); Merrythought Ltd., Two *Dwarfs* from Walt Disney's film *Snow White and the Seven Dwarfs* 99 (c); Villy Nielsen A/S, *Judith Mother and Baby* 129 (tc); Royal Doulton Limited, 124, 125: these items are no longer made by the Company, having been discontinued in 1985.

THE COMMISSIONED PHOTOGRAPHS

All photographs by **Matthew Ward**, except: **Lynton Gardiner** 1 (c), 3 (c), 6 (l, r), 9 (tl), 14, 15 (tl, bl), 22, 23 (c, br), 26, 27, 32, 33, 42 (br), 43, 44, 45 (except tl), 46, 47 (except br), 48, 49 (except c), 50, 51 (except tl, bl), 74 (r), 75, 88, 90, 91 (except tr), 92, 93 (except tl), 97, 99 (tr), 101 (tl, tr), 104 (br), 105 (br), 106, 107 (tr), 138 (cl), 139 (br), 156 (bl), 157 (tl); and **Tony Sandin** 101 (bl).

THE COMMISSIONED ILLUSTRATIONS

The decorative watercolor, gouache, and airbrush on paper illustrations are the work of Marc Adams.
The decorative line devices and the drawing of a hand, used to indicate doll height, are the work of Stephen Dew.

ARCHIVE PICTURE CREDITS

Ashmolean Museum, Oxford 11 (br); Bridgeman Art Library 7 (bl); by kind permission of the Chairman, Mr. Mohamed Al Fayed, Harrods Ltd./Reuters 110 (b); Ursula Gander-Bonet 53; The Hulton Picture Company 31; Japan National Tourist Organization 131 (tl); Oscar and Peter Johnson 8 (c); Maidstone Museum and Art Gallery 43; Mary Evans Picture Library 89; Retrograph Archive 104 (l); Sotheby's London 52 (bl); by courtesy of the Board of Trustees of the Victoria & Albert Museum 11 (tl).

NOVELTY HAT-DOFFER *Made in England at the end of the 19th century, this sprightly fellow has a ceramic head, with molded and painted hair, and wooden arms and legs. A squeeze of the bellows, housed inside the wire body, activates the dolls arm. Ht: 8in (20cm)*